AF521643

Tug of War:
A Triumph of Faith
Peter Daddone

Mary Ethel,

People like you make Frederick H.S. worth everything. Your willingness to do so much for others is inspirational!

Pete Daddone

Aeron House
Maryland Michigan

Published by Aeron House
P.O. Box 1547
Frederick, MD 21702

ISBN: 0-9666754-0-1

Library of Congress Cataloging Data

Daddone, Peter
Tug of War: A Triumph of Faith
I. Tittle
98-093745

Manufactured in the United States of America

Cover design by Kristi Waters

In my life, I only wish to make two people proud of me, my wife and son. I hope that I can someday see my son be as proud of me as I am of him. I would like to dedicate my first work to a variety of people. First, my wife, who has made many immeasureable sacrifices to see a dream of mine come true. Through her, I know what love is. Next, my parents and my grandmother, who have taught me that life is the most precious, priceless commodity to have. Also, my godmother Maria Dufrense, who has shown me the importance of fighting every day of our lives to overcome adversity, to find happiness on the other side of every down turn, and the reward that comes when triumphant over those adversities. One day at a time Maria.

My thanks to my high school English teacher, Marianne Ferreri. Those many hours in the hall reading a student's angst didn't go to waste.

Perhaps most importantly, this novel is dedicated to all of those who have lost their church in the arson attacks. Thank you for your faith. You are a shinning example of goodness in this world. The example of faith in your ability to overcome a devestating adversity is an example that can't be ignored. I only hope that I was able to capture a small measure of your greatness.

Finally, a very special thank you goes out to Ian Riley. The production of this novel would not have been possible with out his technical assistance.

"When my spirit within me languishes
it is thou who knowest my wary!"(Ps. 142:3.)

"The stone which the builders rejected
has become the chief cornerstone." (Ps. 118:22.)

Tug of War

The waitress poured the man another cup of coffee, his third cup in less than an hour. He stared at his cup never acknowledging that he was aware of her presence. She had seen this type of behavior so many times on the night shift. All the losers sitting alone at the counter, wondering what went wrong in their lives. Some had even taken their own lives shortly after leaving the counter. Twice she'd served the last cups of coffee to patrons who'd then gone back to their cars, pulled a gun out of their glove compartment, and ended their miserable lives. This man sitting at the counter seemed to agonize over something.

The man wore a wrinkled tee shirt and shorts. He reread a crumpled newspaper article many times. The newspaper article was about a town in Alabama, his destination. He wasn't sure why he was stuck at this all night diner in Hagerstown, Maryland. He wasn't sure why he was going specifically to this town to help rebuild their church. He sat at the counter sipping his cup of coffee, reliving the events that brought him to this point...

The bar was busy with Friday afternoon happy hour patrons. It was warm and muggy and altogether uncomfortable for the patrons outside by the lake. Like most summer days in western Maryland, the sun beat on relentlessly in the late afternoon. The people seemed to revel in or completely ignore the heat.

For most it was an opportunity to wash away a long and frustrating week, and they sat on the stools and drowned the week away as quickly as possible in the ice cold alcohol that flowed from the bartender's hands. The bartender was the patrons' savior. Patrons placed credit cards on the bar rail and left them there and never once glanced at the receipt they were signing. They were only too glad to pay any price for the sweet salvation that Friday night happy hour gave them.

Lost in the school of happy hour patrons was Dan Meridian. Dan was thirty-four years old. On the surface of Dan's life, he had everything any one person could want. His wife was extremely intelligent and had aged well. He had two healthy and beautiful children, Jack and Francesca. Both were past the "terrible twos," and recently he'd been able to take them on trips to baseball games, movie theaters, and even golf courses. Some would say that Dan had life in the palm of his hand,

and until six months before, Dan wouldn't have been able to think of one thing to prove them wrong.

Dan had retained most of his handsomeness, though not most of his hair. He was almost completely bald and kept his hair close-cropped. He decided long ago not to try to hide his baldness. He had tried cutting edge methods to replace his hair. After six months of using them, he abruptly stopped when he woke up one morning after falling asleep upright against the bedroom wall and discovered that the medicine had peeled the paint off. He decided at that moment that he would be bald forever. This decision allowed him to acknowledge fate and all of the scary possibilities it would bring. He was no longer worried about death.

Dan was a high school teacher. He'd witnessed many aspects of teenage life from that vantage point. He'd seen kids strung out on just about every drug imaginable. He'd seen the awful result of the "huffing" craze. He'd seen kids overcome these addictions and many other handicaps to go on to do great things. He'd seen people better and worse off than himself. He was the middle of the road. He never had enough money to do everything, and sometimes he never had enough money to pay the bills; but, he could've been content with his life. He wasn't.

He sat on his stool in his khaki shorts and maroon polo shirt and tried to bury the heat in the cool beer that ran down his throat. He was there like the rest of them, only he was trying to drown out the past six months of his life. He'd told himself over and over again that he was a fool, that life was great for him, and that he'd been dealt a good hand by fate.

He'd somehow convinced himself that he was falling out of love. This lack of love included his wife, although anyone who knew his wife would call him a fool if he said so out loud. He no longer loved any aspect of his life. A man who'd worked very hard at his job, he suddenly stopped preparing for it. A man who always had time to talk with students and could be seen playing basketball with them after school, he never showed up anymore. A man who coached two sports, wrestling and baseball, who prided himself on his physical conditioning, he had suddenly stopped working out and gained ten pounds. No, something was wrong with Dan Meridian's life. He was pounding down the beers but for the life of him, he couldn't figure out why.

The beer went to his head. He hadn't been a beer drinker since college. In those days, he could easily have had a six pack with a bunch of friends and still hit a bull's eye on a dart board. He couldn't think about himself. Every time he tried to think about himself, he had to do something for someone else. It was either giving up all his free time or yelling at the kids. It was either talking to the day care people about his kids or to the teachers about testing for Special Education modifications. Always meetings, always something. He'd been married for nearly ten years, and for the last seven years it was a life filled with a selfless nature that was spawned out of necessity. The bartender gave him his third beer, and he focused his attention on the person he'd come to the bar with.

"I was very impressed with you."

He was snapped out of his daydream by her sultry voice.

The music was blaring and he noticed for the first time how packed the bar was. Her eyes were steel blue, highlighted by the short, tight, gold summer dress she wore. The light breeze lifted her summer dress a few tantalizing inches up her thigh.

She moved closer to him after the breeze had died away, inviting him to observe the other aspects of her body closely. She was his student teacher, a twenty-two-year-old coed from the University of Maryland. They'd shared the classroom and students for the past ten weeks. He could close his eyes, as he would often do at night, and still see every curve, every lock of hair, and the small tattoo on the back of her shoulder.

He knew all about her because he'd "accidentally" seen the black and white art photos of her nude body that she left in the journal she was to keep about her student teaching. She blushed in apparent embarrassment when he gave her the book back, but those same pictures appeared in the book a week later before they finally disappeared. He knew her because he'd studied her, every inch of her. He knew without even looking at the sun dress that it had two tiny strings tied at the shoulder blades and a zipper in the back. How many times he'd imagined opening that zipper. As the beer swelled his head, he knew he'd have his chance tonight.

He could tell that she was not wearing a bra. The

breeze blew up again. He swore to himself that she wasn't wearing any panties either. Suddenly, the heat rushed on him. He became dizzy and nauseous.

"I... have to go to the bathroom," he said weakly.

She smiled at him. His heart sank as he weaved his way through the crowd to the bathroom. He splashed the cool water on his face. He dried his hands off, took a deep breath, and succumbed to the inevitable. He fought his way back to his bar stool where she was waiting for him. Her right leg was raised against the bar and her elbows rested comfortably on the bar rail.

"I was amazed at how well you were able to handle the kids," she said.

He just nodded. He didn't know what she was talking about because he'd hardly ever known there were kids at all in his classroom. She fluttered her eyes and he felt the wave of them crash over him. She kept on swaying her hips ever so slightly to the rhythm of the music, inviting him in that teasing way to come in. He needed no more encouragement. He'd resisted all of her offers in the past. She'd invited him to basketball games at school, to dinner at her apartment close by, but he'd refused them all until now. He couldn't think straight. It wasn't because of the alcohol. He was wrestling with something deep within his soul, and it had divided his attention.

As the bartender brought Dan's fourth beer, he knew if he drank it, he'd enter the world of inebriation and possibly places not known to him for a long time. As he sipped the beer, he knew he'd soon be in a world of trouble.

He wasn't sure if he was running away from it or welcoming it. He knew he was running from something, but for the life of him he didn't know what. But a part of him was just hoping, praying, that he would wind up at her apartment.

They drove together to work, and often he would be left standing in the hallway as she finished dressing. It drove him crazy. His responsible side knew if he ravished her, they would be late and he'd be disciplined, but another side of him didn't give a damn. He always gave in to the sensible side.

He was not in this reality. He vaguely saw her laughing at something idiotic he must've said. For sure it was some bland joke. He told those often enough, and she laughed long and hard at them. This attracted him to her immensely.

He saw her jerk her head backward having a good laugh; he saw the nape of her neck. He wondered: "What would it be like to see her writhe like that at the pleasure I was giving her?" He knew then that he was doing exactly that. He was pleasing her. He was looking over her body. She saw him do this and took pleasure in it. She had command over him, she was in control, and she loved it. She knew she had him, and it gave her pleasure; just like when he was teaching and he looked at her in the back of the classroom. She didn't pretend not to notice. She absorbed his gaze and implored him with her eyes to look more closely. They locked in on his soul and he did whatever they told him to do. He'd resisted all attempts to do something with her, and now he was drinking beers and losing control of his senses, and he was about to give himself up to her.

She was talking, but he didn't hear her. He was remembering when she walked into his room for the first time. The flatness of her stomach and her thin thighs almost drove him out of his mind. Her tatoo came into his consciousness, a small caracature whose pitchfork left little doubt as to its identitiy. He came back to reality with a pop and ordered his fifth beer. That sensible part of his mind had ordered him to stop, but he brushed these thoughts aside and took a long swallow of ice cold beer.

He looked at the quarter-empty bottle. He knew that if he drank this beer, this one last beer, he would surely be heading down that road that led to her apartment. He looked around the bar now. Laughter surrounded him. He wanted to be that happy about life. He took another long swallow and fell into the abyss. The absolute passion had long since been gone from all aspects of his life, and he was looking for it. It was a part of him. Passion had been his life in one form or another, and now it was less than an arm's reach away. The passion that he and his wife had transformed into the white-hot anger and arguments about love and trustworthiness. None of that was in Dan Meridian, and it scared the hell out of him.

At first, he rationalized that he was with this woman because he wanted to see if he still had the old flame, to see if he could attract someone. He had often looked in the mirror and seen a balding runt of a man and thought there was nothing left for him. In what seemed a heartbeat, the beer was gone. The drunkenness engulfed him like the winds of a hurricane. Suddenly, she was next to him. She was rubbing against him in the crowded bar. He could feel the naked softness of her thighs against his.

She moved up to him with the gracefulness of an approaching breeze.

"This is not the proper way for me to repay you for all of your help this year. I really appreciate everything you've done for me. I wish there was some other way I could repay you."

He smiled and said one of those stupid jokes again.

She laughed. "I've been practicing my gourmet cooking. Why don't we go back to my place and let me fix you a nice dinner?"

He felt passion then, and it was white hot. The decision had come. It had taken ten weeks of thinking about it, and now she was leaning off her bar stool toward him. He couldn't avoid it any longer. He was in familiar territory now. The split-second decision. He got a whiff of her perfume and it steadied him. The passion had enveloped him, but the other side of his brain began to function again and it was echoing to him like a voice at the end of a tunnel. He saw the dreamy blue eyes and felt the soft skin. Everything about her was about to take possession of his soul, but the voice in the tunnel grew louder, and once again he couldn't hear what he was saying. There was disappointment in her eyes and her face reddened.

Moments later they were at the driveway to her

apartment and she was getting out. Instead of walking to her door, she did an about-face and headed back to his car. She grabbed him and kissed him hungrily on the lips. He didn't pull away. After a long moment, with the wave of passion hovering over him, she pulled away, and his heart sank.

"I want you, Dan. I yearn for you. You can have me anytime. I'll be here. You know where to find me." She turned and walked away.

Her walk lured him, dared him, to follow. He ached for her, and he got out of the car and ran for her. When he turned her around, she was crying.

"I have never loved so much and gotten so little," she said as he held her shoulders.

"Debbie, if I give you myself, it wouldn't be all of me. I have to make a decision. You either get all of me or none of me. Don't you want all of me?"

She smiled then and her eyes returned to normal. "Yes, of course I do."

"Well, if I go to you, I want to go for good. Can you handle that? I'm not looking for permanence, I just want to give all of myself to you, and in order for me to do that, I have to make a very painful decision. I don't want anything to cloud that decision. Do you understand?"

She looked at him in awe. Her love for him had reached new heights. "You'd give up so much for me?"

"I honestly don't know. That's why I can't go to you now." He let go of her. "I don't know how long it'll take. I've lost something, but I don't know what it is or how to reclaim it. When I do find it, I'm not sure if it'll lead me to your door."

She smiled. "Do whatever it takes. I hope it leads you to me, but I also hope you find what you're looking for."

He smiled. The inebriation had worn down, but the anxiety of his sense of helplessness didn't cease. "I honestly can't figure out what I need. I don't know how to find the road I need to take to find myself. I don't know where to start."

Chapter 2

It was late in the evening when he got home. He'd driven practically to western Pennsylvania and back again. He didn't know what he was running to, but he knew he had to find out before it tore him apart. He didn't go to bed when he got home but stayed at the kitchen table nursing a beer. He didn't look at his wife, didn't even acknowledge she was there.

"Did you sleep with her?" she asked as calmly as if she were asking him to pass the salt.

He turned to her just as calmly, almost as slowly. "No, but I almost did."

She got up and left the table. He didn't try to get her back, didn't try to explain. He couldn't give a damn what she thought. He was tired of caring. He was tired of everyone relying on him.

For two weeks after school ended, he had barely

talked to his wife. Neither spoke to the other. Dan thought it was odd there was no tension around this. It was almost as if they both looked forward to the silence. His children had gone to various summer activities. Jack, his oldest was in camp, and Francesca was at her grandparents' house.

Dan wanted Debbie, but he methodically analyzed his life and discovered there was no order. There was nothing for him to hang his hopes on. Sadly, he discovered that it really wasn't about wanting to take a mistress, but was really an excuse to further put off what was boiling inside him, something he couldn't place his finger on, but knew he'd have to discover if he would ever be able to chose the right path.

As the middle of July approached, Dan thought he needed to get away from his surroundings. He needed to find some place where he could try to sort out his life and find out in which direction he should go.

Late one night, just three days before the Olympics were to begin, his wife moved close to him. It had been the first time she'd touched him in some time. She held his hand. "I think you should go some place for a while. You need to get over something, get something I can't give you. I don't know if you love me anymore."

He couldn't see in the darkness, but he knew tears were flowing down her cheeks. He felt close to her and saw some of the love for her return. He started to say something, but she cut him off.

"No. Don't say anything. I believe you when you said you didn't make love to that girl. I didn't at first, but I do now. I've watched you mope around this house. I think you must get out of this house. You're going to have to find your way again somehow." Tears flowed freely down her face. "I don't know where we lost it, but we have. I hope we can find it again because I'd hate to lose you, but I want all of you or I don't want any of you."

All the next day, he hung around the house shrowded in his gloom. He sat at the kitchen table with the thought of his failure. He may've thrown a perfectly good life away because he was going through some type of "crisis." Had he already gone down some wrong path? Had the choice already been made for him? That would be worse, he thought to himself, if somebody, or something else had made the decision for him.

He sat in the kitchen for a long time without moving. He wasn't a religious man. He hadn't been in a church more than twice in any given year. He was a Catholic, and he thought it might be a good time to talk with a priest. He was confused because he believed in God, but not all of the principles of his faith. He'd never sought out a priest or holy man before. His wife was his God, his confessional, his advisor. Now he'd pushed her further away than she was willing to accept. He sat alone tangled up in his web of thoughts.

At last he picked up the paper, as if trying to read would give him an answer. He read the entire paper, all of the sections, even the obituaries. There, right there in front of him were at least half a dozen people who'd gladly trade places with him in a second. He hoped that he would gain some measure of appreciation for his life after reading the obituaries, but it didn't work. Desperation slowly sank in. He read the front page article a second time. It focused on the Southern church bombings. Being a sport enthusiast enabled him to already know the problem long before it became front page headlines. He had read about a famous football player's drive to end this hatred over a year ago. Now more than seventy churches had been burned, mostly in the South. The article focused on how the Olympics would be in the South soon and how the hope that the unification of a world sporting event would somehow stamp out the hatred.

Dan thought as he read the article, "Sports can't unify a people filled with hatred for one another. It can't provide hope. In sports it's not the effort that counts, it's whether you win or lose. If you win, you're a winner. If you lose, you're a loser."

The article then focused on a small town in Alabama. This town was attempting to work together, over seemingly impossible odds, to erect another church near the site of the original one. The article focused on a local white landowner whose great grandfather owned slaves in that state and who'd donated the extra hundred yards of land to accomodate the area of the new church. The article quoted the landowner saying he was giving back something that was "long overdue." In addition, the article told about a restaurant owner in the next town, whose father refused to let black people in his restaurant in the early sixties, who was now catering meals at no charge for the workers. The entire community pulled together in an attempt to erase the work of hatred.

The article didn't have a happy ending. The entire town of Spleen was below the poverty line. There was a lack of funds, and just as important, a lack of hands to help build the church. The article ended with a seemingly optimistic quote from the minister of the church, John Freeman, who predicted that God would save the church. There was a picture of Freeman, the blackened remains of the church in the background, and the quarter finished new church behind it.

Dan looked at the picture of Freeman for a long time. At last it came to him. He ran upstairs and began to pack, all the time trying to explain to his wife what he was going to do. She looked at him quizically but said nothing. He put the duffel bag full of clothes in his blue 1991 Ford Escort, waved a short goodbye to his wife, and drove headlong into the setting mid-July sun.

Chapter 3

Dan paid the waitress for the coffee. As the sun set along Interstate Seventy, Dan Meridian had no idea what he was doing. His sudden enthusiasm to go to Alabama and help some people build a church had begun to lose its excitement. Once again he became selfish and began to think of heading east instead and spending a few weeks relaxing on the beach in Ocean City. He'd relax for hours there and just think about what decision he needed to make. He'd come back at the end of July, his kids would be just coming home then, and he would be ready to announce his intentions.

He nursed a cup of black coffee at another all night truck stop at the edge of the Interstate Eighty-One junction. As the aging waitress poured him another cup, he'd pretty much decided that was exactly what he would do. Then his mind flashed back to the picture of John Freeman again. He was riveted to that image and he didn't know why. The vibrant eyes seemed to gravitate toward him, and he couldn't look away from them. Fifteen minutes had gone by without him noticing.

Two hours later he was again agonizing over his decision to head south. He'd head down Interstate Eighty-One toward Roanoke, Virginia and eventually wind up in Spleen, Alabama. He cursed himself for wasting so much time and made up his mind to head home with the intent of going toward the damn beach. He veered off suddenly into an emergency vehicle U-turn island. He made his turn and began to accelerate up Eighty-One North.

He didn't get very far before a police cruiser flashed its lights. He eased to the side of the road, thoroughly upset at himself. He fumbled for his wallet, still cursing himself up and down. Dan had his license and registration out before the officer got to his car. In fact, the officer hadn't come out of his car yet. Five minutes went by and still, no officer.

Dan hissed under his breath. "God damn, I hate it when they pull that crap." He knew the routine and hated it. "Why is it that officers purposefully spend twenty to thirty minutes giving you a ticket when you know damn well it takes them less than five to write it up?"

Sure enough, after the seventh minute, the police officer exited his car. He approached with a slow, laid back stride as Dan put his arms on the steering wheel.

"Sir, did you know that you made a U-turn back there illegally?"

"Yes officer."

"Sir, do you have an emergency?"

Dan stopped. It took a long time to think about it. In a flash all of the events rushed forward like a kaleidoscope of colors. It was indeed an emergency. It wasn't the kind of emergency the policeman was asking him about, but it was still an emergency. Dan realized that his very soul was at stake. This was a fight for the very essence of his being, a war within himself. The lights rotated around the emptiness of his car. His mind was only dimly aware of the huge battle it had before it. Finally, after careful consideration, he realized that he had an emergency of the soul. He still couldn't quite place his finger on it, but he realized that this emergency wouldn't be solved on some beach. Like everything else in his life, he was running away from what could save him. His heart leaped at the realization. A smile came across his lips. The officer had no idea how to read it. Dan was certain now that the only way he would solve this mystery, and pick which road to take in his life, lay within the eyes and soul of John Freeman.

"No officer, no emergency," was Dan's only reply.

He looked at the ticket as the officer headed toward his car. The ticket was a seventy-five dollar fine. He could write a check within fifteen days or appeal the ticket and appear in court in two weeks. The court location was in Middletown, Virginia. He got off the first ramp and returned to Eighty-One South. He hummed softly to himself as the music from the radio broke the monotonous journey south.

At about five o'clock in the morning, he pulled into a truck stop near Waynesboro. He ate a hearty breakfast. He was starving, having not eaten in over a day. After his second breakfast and a third cup of coffee, he felt wonderfully alive, although he knew it was an artificial high set off by the coffee and sugar. He drove another three hours, and by late morning he was in Roanoke and exhausted. There, he checked into a motel, and without removing any of his clothes, fell asleep.

He had a dream. He saw a black man with ugly scars on the right side of his face and hands. The man was smiling at him. Dan tried to run. Everywhere he turned, the man was there, beckoning him toward some place dark and unknown.

Dan woke up with a start, the dream half finished. He took off his shirt and was about to take a shower when he heard children's laughter from outside. He opened the window blinds and saw some children playing in the pool. He smiled, grabbed his shirt and towel, and headed for the pool. He dove into the choppy water and swam for about half an hour, spending most of the time floating effortlessly. The sleep and swim had done wonders for him. For the first time since he'd left home, he was looking forward to his trip.

He showered the chlorine off, pulled on a clean pair of shorts, shirt, and socks from his duffel bag, and tossed the wet set in a plastic bag provided by the hotel. He checked out and had dinner in the motel's restaurant . In the dusk of a new evening, Dan continued his journey to Spleen, Alabama with a sense of longing. He used to be a man driven by goals. He'd set them in front of him like stepping stones. He subscribed to a philosophy of will power and discipline and followed that path with steely determination.

As he pulled the car back onto Eighty-One South, he felt invigorated by a new goal. It wasn't much, but it was a stepping stone.

Chapter 4

Dan hit a thunderstorm at the Tennessee border. He passed Kingsport and stopped in a little town. It was late in the evening, and he decided to stop for a cup of coffee. He found a small rundown cafe open, and a waitress as old as the ancient Formica counter top served him and disappeared. It took over an hour for the storms to pass, but the waitress was still nowhere in sight. Eager to get back on the road, Dan gave up. He left a five dollar bill on the table, leaned over the counter, poured himself a cup of coffee in a large Styrofoam cup, and walked out.

Once back on the road, he continued on Eighty-One South until he approached Knoxville. He stopped at another truck stop. A young waitress, who got more than her share of looks from the pot-bellied truck drivers, poured him a second cup of coffee. She smiled at him through cavity stricken teeth. Dan guessed that she couldn't have been more than eighteen. Her eyes were already bloodshot. He saw that she would age much more quickly than she should. He pulled out a map and figured out that he would need to take Forty West to Seventy South in order to get to the Alabama border.

As he prepared to leave, he stopped and looked at a new television in the corner. He joined the truck drivers watching the opening ceremonies of the Olympics. He watched in awe as the Olympic torch, the symbol of unification in sports, took the last few steps of its long journey from across the world. He watched as the spirit of the games began to envelop the patrons and the torch bearer held it up for the spectators and athletes to see. Then, after the slightest of hesitations, the small torch became an awesome ball of flame that would burn brightly throughout the Olympics. The flame expanded and burned brilliantly in the Atlanta evening.

Ten minutes later, Dan left. The patrons were talking with each other, when only moments before they were sitting at their stools with invisible walls surrounding them. Dan wondered if sports could unify a people, bring them together. As he drove toward Alabama, he dismissed the thought and pulled himself back toward his goal of getting to Spleen by the next afternoon. He checked his watch and pressed harder on the gas, unsure if he'd make it.

The sky changed color slowly before his eyes. In another hour, he wouldn't need his lights. He thought he had a good shot of making it by noon. He stopped at yet another truck stop near Gadsden to fill up. While he was paying, he noticed the station littered with Olympic hats, shirts, pins, and programs. He realized how close he was to Atlanta. At Gadsden he turned west onto Two-Seventy-Eight. Past Cullman, he turned right onto a small road, Route Seven, and then an even smaller road ten miles later. There were no signs or directions. He saw many billboards and road signs proclaiming the Lord, and even three crosses and the words "Jesus sacrificed his life for you, what are you doing about it?"

The roads became barely discernable. He bought a local map and pulled off to the side of the road and began to study it. His back began to bead sweat. He was completely lost. His worst fear, his utter nightmare, the thing he dreaded most in the world, suddenly became a realization. He hated getting lost, and now he had no place to go. He decided suddenly to turn back and retrace his steps. Soon, he found Route Seven again. In a panic, he was prepared to give up his whole journey, but he'd already come so far.

He pulled off the side of the road and got out of his car to stretch. He was sure Spleen was somewhere close by. He walked a few paces up and down the road. He wanted to go further down the road to try to find Spleen, but his fear was too great. He looked at the local maps again. There were more spots outlined for churches than there were for roads.

Something clicked in his mind. He jumped back into his car, reached behind the back seat, and pulled out a spray can. It was artificial limestone. He was a baseball coach, and he had six cans in his back seat to draw lines for games. He put the key in the ignition and excitedly drove back to the turn-off. He stopped, hauled himself out of the car, and drew a giant X on the side of the road. He continued to drive along to where he thought Spleen might be. He remembered the story of Hansel and Gretel, and now he was doing what they did; he was laying down markers so that he could find his way back out if he had to by retracing his steps.

About a half hour later, he found himself off the road completely. He was traveling on dirt roads, and he wasn't sure how much more his car would be able to take. He was about done with his first can, and the fields of cotton had no end in sight. As he turned a roughed-out corner, the cotton fields gave way and he saw a church ahead. He pulled up to it, only to discover that the church wasn't on the map. His shirt was drenched in sweat as he turned off the car. It wasn't even the heat of the day. He climbed up the short steps of the church and entered. The shade of the interior barely relieved the heat.

"Hello!" he shouted, but no one answered.

He heard humming in the back of the church and approached the noise. As the noise grew louder, he perceived it to be an air conditioner. As he got closer, he heard a television as well. His hopes grew as he felt someone was inside. He approached the door and knocked on it. A few moments later, he heard footsteps and then the door opened and the cool air swept over him like a tidal wave.

"Who are you?" the man asked.

"My name is Dan Meridian, Father. I need some help."

"That's why we're in business. Come in, you're letting all the cool air out."

The room had warmed up considerably in the short time the door was open. Dan entered a small room. There was a small bed, a kitchen, and a television on the counter. A small bookcase was in the corner, half full of tattered books, half full of canned goods.

"Reverend Harper's my name. What can I do for you today, sir?"

"I'm lost."

Dan pulled his attention from the Reverend

to the television. A talk show was on, but the volume was too low for him to recognize the subject.

"Many of us get lost along the long path, Son."

"How can you get lost? You live here."

"We all have such a long journey to make that we are bound to lose our way sometimes."

Dan stood motionless. Then he caught on. "Reverend..."

"Call me Jesse."

Dan nodded. "I didn't mean it like that." He pointed to the door. "Out there. I'm driving, and I'm lost. I was wondering if you could help me."

Jesse Harper let out a deep laugh. He was well over six feet and over two hundred and fifty pounds. His hair was completely gray. His thick dark-skinned neck bulged out of his shirt collar even though it was unbuttoned at the top. "I'm sorry, I guess I just assumed. Nobody comes in here much except to ask for forgiveness, talk to me, or sit in front of one of the four air conditioners in the town. Can I offer you some lemonade?"

"Sure." Dan hadn't realized how thirsty he was. Neither of them spoke as he drained down three quarters of the ice cold liquid.

"I should've picked up the lack of an accent," Jesse said.

Dan shrugged. "To be honest, you don't have

one either."

"Went to school and lived in New York for a dozen years. I guess I lost the Southern drawl somewhere along the line."

"Where did you go to school?"

"Columbia."

"Really?"

"You want to ask me why I'm here," Jesse said.

"Forgive me. You've been very hospitable. I didn't mean to upset you."

"Don't worry about it, son. Everyone asks. I was born in Alabama. I went to New York to get away from the racism and hatred. Got a great education. Worked for one of the largest advertising agencies on the planet. Came up with some great ads, too."

Harper shrugged the memories away. "Well anyway, I never got higher than an account executive even though people with less knowledge and time in the company did. My father died and willed me some land behind the church with the house. I sold my belongings, came down here, and went to divinity school to become a Reverend. They made me pastor of this fine church here. I realized a long time ago that it doesn't matter where you go, hatred and bigotry will always be there. The only place where I have yet to find that is in this church right here."

Dan sat in silence for a while. He furthered the silence by gulping the last of his lemonade.

Jesse filled his glass again and handed it to Dan.

"So, young man, how can I help you?"

"It's kind of hard to explain. I live in Maryland, and I have come down here because I read an article about how Spleen, Alabama has a church that was fire-bombed and needs repairing. I've decided, and I don't know if this is plain stupid or not, but I came down here to help out if I could. So what I need to know is how the he... How the heck do I get to Spleen, Alabama?"

Jesse breathed in deeply and laughed. "Son, you're in Spleen!"

Dan looked confused. "But where is the town?"

Jesse never stopped laughing. "There isn't much of a town. It's at the bottom of the hill. There is even a street in better shape than the one you're on now. The church you're looking for is about two miles from here. Just go to the end of the town; it's not that far. Make a right at the soda fountain restaurant. At the end of that road you'll see the church. You can't miss it."

Dan was incredibly relieved. "Oh, this is great! I was so worried. I thought I would never get here!"

"Well now, hold on. This isn't going to be a great place to hang around, you know. There really isn't any place to stay in town. I think you're going to find Spleen, Alabama a bit different. Things really don't change around here."

"Do people take kindly to strangers?"

"In a lot of ways, we're just like the stereotypical South, but we're different as well. We don't get many visitors. I think you'll find that we enjoy the company of good folks every once in a while."

Dan wanted to stay, but it was already past noon and he was eager to finally arrive at his destination. He was torn because it was brutally hot outside and Jesse Harper had an air conditioner.

Two more glasses of lemonade later, Dan found himself in the middle of the swarming heat again.

Jesse Harper hurriedly waved him on, "Come on back and visit before you leave."

Dan put the car into drive, slowly negotiating the large pot holes and mud. As it turned out, he'd come to Spleen through the back way. By the time he got to the bottom of the hill, a few rundown businesses jutted out from either side. The main street was an old dusty back road. The mud was caked down hard by the years of use. It had a smooth white finish to it. A few rusted vehicles eased on ahead of him, leaving small dust trails.

The first two stores on the "main strip" were indiscernible. The outlines of signs showed on the weather-beaten front, but the signs had disappeared. Father Time hadn't been kind to Spleen. Both stores were open, much to Dan's surprise. The next two stores had signs, but they were barely legible. One was the town grocery store, the other a hunting supply store. The next two stores were newer. One looked as if it'd been painted in the last few years. This was the town's soda fountain restaurant.

Dan stopped the car and pulled into an unmarked parking space. He got out and walked into the soda fountain restaurant. The decor was old, contradicting the newness outside. The black and white linoleum tile was completely faded in many areas. As soon as he walked in, he was confronted by a huge oak counter top with soda fountain taps on either side and an ice cream cooler in the center. Behind the bar were hundreds of different-sized glass mugs. All aspects of the restaurant had the appearance of being scrubbed, cared for, and cleaned much too often.

A strikingly beautiful girl with amazingly dark skin and long straightened hair tied up in a bandanna was rinsing and drying a glass. She looked up, surprised. He smiled and nodded. She smiled back but stood still, letting the dripping mug get the bottom of her blouse wet. A radio blared the deep sultry blues of Albert King. The restaurant to Dan's right was half full of customers. They were all in various stages of eating or ordering, and all eyes were on him.

"Hello, my name is Dan Meridian. I'm from Maryland. I came in for a drink." He fumbled with his hands, and then decided to put them in his pockets.

"You lost or something?" the beautiful woman behind the counter said.

Dan moved forward and eased himself onto one of the few empty stools at the bar.

"Well, I hope not. I mean I came down here because I heard that you were fixing a church, and I was hoping I could help."

There was a long, awkward pause. The beautiful woman continued to look at him as if he were a curiosity behind the bars in a zoo.

"That it? You came all the way from Maryland to help fix the church?"

She had a very thick Southern accent, and he guessed she'd been living in Spleen all her life. She looked to be about his age. She was tall and slender and had the biggest onyx eyes he'd ever seen.

"Well, yes. Oh, and to try your root beer float."

A few of the patrons got a chuckle out of that, and many of the clientele began to eat again. Conversation began to raise in volume. Dan thought some of it no doubt was about him. The woman smiled and seemed to look at him as a person. She prepared the float. He put two singles on the table, and she brought him his change. She leaned over the counter, moving closer to him. She seemed to take him all in, to scrutinize him. He sat there staring back at her.

"Well, you going try it?"

"Oh, sorry."

"Mayella takes a great deal of pride in her work," an old man sitting near him said with a smile. The float was so thick he had trouble getting the liquid up the straw. His senses were attacked with the great taste. He felt as if he'd indeed transcended time.

"Unbelievable," he managed to gasp after his first sip.

She smiled and left him to tend to another customer. Then she turned toward him. "Are you sure that's all you're here for is to help the church?"

"Yes." He managed to say between slurps of the root beer.

"Good. Reverend Freeman is there now. You can meet him there. The church is about a mile away. Make a right at the end of the block and stay on the road until you see the church."

"Thank you." Dan walked out the door into the Alabama heat. He wondered if he would ever get used to the oppressiveness of it.

Chapter 5

Dan left the old restaurant soaked in sweat. There was no air conditioning in the store and the heat was nearly unbearable. He got in his car, cursed at the intense heat that singed his fingertips when he touched the steering wheel, and continued on to his destination.

The last two shops on the main street were just as rundown as the previous ones. There was a store with some out of date fashions hanging in the window and some old games and household supplies. Some pictures, dog eared and faded, hung in the window, giving a hint to the last time the window had been changed. This was by far the largest store in the small main street of town. Through all the stores, there wasn't a hint that the Olympics were occurring just one state over. It was as if America had forgotten Spleen ever existed. It seemed as if Spleen was an important town once, but through the evolution of America, it had simply stopped being useful.

Dan saw an old train station, out of use for a long time. The growth among the railroad ties indicated that a train had once come to the town of Spleen, but had long ago ceased its route. Spleen was literally cut off from the rest of America. From the small hills surrounding it to the cotton fields that hid it from view, Spleen was a lost town.

The view of the charred out remains of the church caught his eye. A few buttresses remained, but other than that, he'd have hardly known a building once stood there. About fifty yards to the right, a half dozen people were working on laying the foundation of what Dan assumed would be the new church. Dan couldn't see the faces of the people, but he could tell there were both black and white workers .

He eased his car slowly off the side and toward a ditch. He put on his emergency brake so the car wouldn't slide further into the ditch. He eased out of the car. He felt queasy. His hands began to sweat, but it wasn't from the heat. It was from the nervousness of trying to explain just one more time, and to the most important people of all, what he was doing here. Dan felt as if this was an important test, and he wasn't sure if he would pass.

A man saw him come up the grass toward the construction site and began to walk toward him. As Dan got closer to the construction site, he noticed four more people were sitting under a tent. Some were eating, others were barbecuing. The man, important-looking in posture and appearance, was coming closer and Dan could see his face. It was kindly, but one of concern. Its dark features were contrasted by a small thicket of graying hair. The right side of his face was scarred. It should have looked horrible, but for some reason the scar didn't intimidate Dan. The man wore work overalls and a short sleeve buttoned down shirt. The shirt was soaked through with perspiration and the overalls were caked with days' old mud and cement. Dan cursed himself for forgetting work clothes, but remembered that he had his fishing overalls and two pairs of jeans in the car.

Dan noticed that the man had the same type of scar along his right hand as well. This was similar to the man in his dream. The man was upon him with a nervous smile and a weak hand shake.

"Can I help you, sir?" The man said with a Southern accent.

"Well, yes you can. My name is Dan Meridian."

"Are you a reporter, sir?"

"No, I'm not."

"Are you part of the Court of Permits Department?"

"No, I'm not."

A broad smile spread across the man's face. "Well then, what can I do for you today?"

"I came to help, sir."

"You came to help? Oh, you mean with the building? Great. We can use all of the help we can get."

They walked toward the work site.

"I hope you don't mind me asking, but you don't sound like you're from around here," the man said.

"I'm from Maryland. I read an article about the church fires which featured a picture of you and of the church here. I'm a teacher. I have the summer off, so I decided to help out if I could."

"Was the picture flattering?"

"Pardon me?" Dan said.

"Did I look good?"

Dan thought for a moment. "I can't recall, to be honest with you."

The man chuckled. "That's good. That's fine. That means it wasn't unflattering."

They walked a few paces closer to the work site and Dan could hear the shouts of orders, and the clanging of equipment.

"I don't think I introduced myself. I'm the pastor of this church. My name is John Freeman."

"Dan."

"Meridian. Right, you said that already." Freeman stopped for a moment. "I didn't mean that in a rude way."

Dan smiled. "No offense taken."

Dan began to walk toward the construction site. He couldn't wait to get to work. He was giddy with anticipation and talked to John Freeman as if he were an old friend.

"Well, at least one good thing has happened with that article. When that reporter came down, this town was real spooked. Then, all of the court people came down fining us and telling us we needed permits. I don't think a single building or house in this town had a permit. Now we finally got everything under control and we thought you were another reporter."

"No, just a regular guy who seeks a direction in life and wants to help."

"Well, I don't know how much direction we can find for you here, but I think we can find plenty of ways for you to help. Have you eaten lunch yet?"

"No."

"Why don't you come join me? Martha Vanguard is serving today, and she makes the best fried chicken in town."

As if on cue, they reached the barbecue tent and a ghostly white woman with short hair and a schoolmarm's sun dress presented a smile and a big basket of fried chicken with a paper towel draped over the top. A second bowl with collard greens and a third bowl with corn on the cob were presented.

All of the workers, including Dan, ate heartily.

During the course of the meal, three of the six workers came and sat down at various times to eat. Dan was introduced to all of them. There was Hal Summers, who'd lived in Spleen all his life and proudly proclaimed to have never left the town. He was in his late sixties and looked to be as strong as an ox. His arms and neck were tanned, but underneath his shirt he was nearly bone white. Jeremiah Jefferson was in his thirties. Sweat shone on his dark skin, and he looked exhausted.

Al Nichols said that Jeremiah was always tired. Al was a portly man who ate quickly and heartily. He had a black mustache and a balding head which was sunburned. He wore suspenders that strained to keep his pants up.

Aretha Freeman seemed to have a perpetual smile. Her long jet black hair blew in the breeze as she served the members of the team. Gill Nouller was the school teacher who worked at the site every single day.

Dan learned that not everyone was able to work every day. In fact, thirty-five members of the town were able to get temporary jobs building roadways for the state. Many of Alabama's state workers had left for Atlanta four months ago, and although the Olympics had already begun, they still remained to finish projects in the vicinity and repair some damaged roads that were caused by springtime floods.

The town of Spleen had a population of one hundred and ninety-eight. Most of the town was over thirty-five years old. The children were bussed one hour to the nearest school system. Most of the town didn't work, but they did tend their own crops for food, and they joined migrant workers occasionally to make money. The people of Spleen weren't used to the type of windfall they'd recently had. With nearly thirty percent of the town work force out of town for months and the usual migrant workers gone to work on plantations and farms for the season, Spleen enjoyed a record high of sixty percent employment. You had to go back fifty-five years to find a better percentage. As a result of all this, the construction site had slightly more than two dozen workers.

They worked in shifts of six, mostly. They came to work once every three days. Most were grateful for something to do, so occasionally the people of the town would work on a near daily basis. Some members worked because they felt the closeness of a small community and reached out to help. Brian Nonmaker was one such person. He was a member of the congregation. He was incredibly strong, deep-voiced, and always singing hollers, traditional blues songs that go back beyond the days of slavery to the very heart of African heritage. Fifteen years ago he was fired from his job as a construction worker for hitting a white man. He came back to Spleen after that incident and was never able to get a job outside of town again. His overalls were torn in several places and his handkerchief was filthy from dirty sweat.

The worker who stood out the most to Dan was Tarsi Jeffries. He was an incredibly athletic sixteen-year-old-boy. He stood nearly six foot two, but he wasn't lanky by any means. He was one of the few children he had seen in the town so far, and the only one working at the site on that day. Beverly Diablue worked in the makeshift kitchen and constantly gave liquids to the working men. She was a widow in her mid-thirties. Her husband had died, along with twenty five other townspeople, when the truck driving them to a migrant job was in a car accident. Finally, Matt Mormberg was as much of a curiosity as Dan Meridian. Matt, like Dan, had decided to come down and help the church. Matt was actually from Kansas City.

They went to work in the afternoon sun. The chance for a late afternoon thunderstorm loomed in the distance as Dan began to work his first shift at the construction site. He changed into his jeans. In fifteen minute intervals, they stopped for a few moments, drank water, and worked some more. By five o'clock in the afternoon, the sun disappeared behind a cluster of angry clouds. The workers stopped, and all were gathered at the tent, which was now flapping in the quickened breeze. They ate quickly, hungrily. They barely spoke to each other.

"Ten minutes." Gil said, and the eaters quickened their pace.

Five minutes later, the paper plates were thrown in the garbage, the remaining food was put back in containers, and the kitchen packed away. The tent, which was flapping crazily, was detached from the poles and placed in the back of a thirty year-old pickup truck, dented and rusted with age. Most of the members waved good bye, and talk of meeting back at nine o'clock in the morning ended as the group scurried back to the dirt road and toward one direction or another. Dan began to move toward his car. He'd forgotten to get directions to a town with a motel in it. Fighting the strong winds, he ran to John Freeman's car, which was the old truck. The rumblings of the thunder and the flashes of lightning were bright and very close.

"Excuse me, Reverend Freeman. You don't happen to know where the nearest hotel is, do you?"

Freeman frowned. "I know one in Spokeen, but that's almost an hour away. I think your best bet will be to stay in town. This is going to be a pretty big thunderstorm." Freeman had to shout his words above the impending storm.

"Why don't you follow us home? We live less than a mile away. You should stay with us."

"I don't want to put you out," Dan said over a bolt of lightning.

"In less than a minute the skies are going to open up, and then you're going to know that there is such a thing as God. I think the best thing for you to do is follow us and let us put you up."

Dan didn't argue anymore. He ran to his car and within seconds was following the old truck down the road.

The storm was huge. The wind blew so mightily that Dan's little car was blowing off its course a bit. The rain fell with the mixture of hail and Dan could barely see the car in front of him.

Almost as soon as the storm started, the truck pulled into another muddy driveway. The house was a bit bigger than some of the others Dan had seen on his way to town, but the condition of the house was the same. There were a few open wounds to the house. The house had a brick bottom, but about two feet above the ground started the shingles. There were numerous spots where the shingles were missing and the paper was flapping loosely. The concrete walkway was cracked and disjointed. The garage door was missing.

The truck pulled into the open bay and Dan pulled in behind outside. Dan got out of the car and ran for the open doorway. Rain stung him like tiny thorns. He ran under the canopy of the garage and shook the water off.

He was soaked. He looked at the smiling faces in front of him. This would become his home for the next two weeks.

Chapter 6

The inside of the home looked much the same as the outside. There was evidence of poverty all over the place. The walls were dirty from years of not being repainted, and the rugs were worn. Still, the home was furnished and cared for. The faded linoleum kitchen floor was polished and completely cleaned. Family heirlooms and antiques decorated the corners of the house. Even the very old aluminum table glistened with the signs of love.

They entered the kitchen and John Freeman pulled out a matchbook and candle. "No sense in even trying the electricity. Our area is always the first to go in a storm."

He motioned Dan to a chair. They all sat down in the evening candlelight as the storm bristled overhead. Dan felt invigorated. He was exhausted by the end of his first day on the job. His limbs had begun to ache with the strain of lifting the cinder blocks and cementing them. Even though it was a short dash from the muddy driveway to the sanctuary of the garage, he'd been doused and felt strangely awake. He listened intently as John talked to him about his house, his family, and his life. Aretha poured him an ice cold glass of homemade iced tea.

"When we were married fifteen years ago, the wedding was just like any other in this town. We're a poor town, and in some ways we're a backward town. Like all towns there's some hatred, but for the most part we've gotten along. Even during the Civil War, we were a town that kept to itself and we were too small to be considered significant. The war and Reconstruction went on without us and that suited us just fine.

"We had a booming period in the forties and fifties. A railroad station was built and the line stopped here. There was a lot of work for everyone because so many young men went off to fight in the war. When they got back, the railroad brought them here, but never returned. The line was shifted and the railroad slowly became obsolete.

"By early nineteen-sixty we were back to being left alone by the rest of the country, and that suited us fine as well. We read in the newspapers and saw on the televisions what was happening to America, the Civil Rights Movement, the protests, the Vietnam War. Occasionally, we were hit with violence or influenced in some way, but eventually our town would go back to normal.

"My family has stayed in this town for as long as the town has existed. People will tell you much more about this town, and you will learn some of it on your own."

Dan took a sip of his iced tea. "I noticed you have quite a lot of antiques here. Are they passed down?"

"Yes, that was what I was trying to get to. I have so much pride in this town that sometimes I get sidetracked trying to tell people about its history." John waved a hand about the rooms in the house.

Dan watched John's face soften as he spoke, watched the wonder in John's expression. He felt a mix of deep appreciation and depression. Memories of his family materialized. He remembered his father. A grim image, shattered recollections of his childhood and nothing more. A man yelling, closing the door, never to return.

John shifted in his seat. "I was taught that it's not how much you have in life, but it's what you do with it. We don't have much in our lives, but we're very proud of what we have done." John got up and walked slowly around the room.

"Most everything in this house has come from some member of our family or from one of our friends."

John touched an antique lamp. "When we were married, as is the tradition of this town, Aretha and I were given a piece of a family's or friend's life. Many of the items you see here were given to us, and they're an important part of that family or friend. They are items that have survived and have been handed down from generation to generation. They represent something far greater than anything we can ever hope for. It is a tradition that has been a part of our community for hundreds of years and was carried across the ocean by the town's founding fathers when they came to this country by force."

Dan thought about his own family. Love was a mirage. Growing up was a case of survival of the fittest. It was a game, and he had thought he had won the game. He thought he had overcome the odds and survived. It was only that his soul was dead.

Dan felt a strange regret. His own wedding had been small, since he'd long been distant from his siblings and father. He wanted to speak, but the look on John's face, the pride, stopped him.

"We work painstakingly hard to maintain the splendor and beauty of our heirlooms. For instance, tomorrow we will use the toaster that's twenty-five years old. As silly as this sounds, we keep it in excellent order, and we will be sad if it's ever broken because it was given to us by a great distant relative who's passed on. The unique thing about each wedding is that each present is wrapped in a cloth and it's the new wife's duty to sew those fabrics into a blanket. When all of the pieces are sewn together, the blanket is placed on the bed of the new couple and stays there for one year. As they wrap themselves in it, the blanket symbolizes the closeness of each other and the closeness of their friends and family. It's a gift that teaches them that poverty is just a word. The blanket is then disassembled and used to wrap the wedding presents given in the years to come. The last is given to the first child on his or her wedding. These are some of the things we do in this town that make us unique, create a special purpose to history. We don't have much in this town, but we do have each other."

Dan was struck suddenly with a powerful sense of respect for the people of this town. His regret was deep within him. His heart sank at this missing piece in his own life. He felt cheated and angry.

"We get most of these traditions from our elders. They keep the heritage of our family intact. They're our link between the past and our future. They help us understand what love is and its importance in life. They have shown us what it felt like when they saw Kennedy assassinated on television, or when they found out that men walked on the moon, or when Martin Luther King was assassinated. They are the link to our heritage, our American version of the African griots, people who were responsible for chronicaling our heritage, our history. Our elders keep an oral history of this town. Our lives are based on history, not just of this town, but of our families and life.

"We're a poor town, but more than half of us have televisions because we love to see what's going on in the world. We don't just pass our history to our children. We pass our feelings about life to our children. It's not uncommon to see four or five families at one home watching television and discussing the significance of what they saw. I know for a fact that we'll all be together watching the Olympics with many of the same people who helped us out today. We will never be so close to the entire world ever again. Some folks give money to children who graduate from college or who get married. We can't give our children such things so we try to give them a piece of our mind, all we know about our heritage, and all that we've experienced in the past. It's been this way since before we were driven to this country for sale."

The thunder overhead had become a distant rumbling. The depression was deep in Dan. He felt he'd moved backward in his desire to find a solution to his problems. Here was a town, a family, which had some enduring customs, and Dan had never really known his family. His father and mother were part of the sixties generation. They married and had children, but never really loved each other. His father, an elevator repairman, fell in love with acid, pot, and the free love that came with it. His mother tried to put on a brave face until he started on cocaine and disappeared. She took her two children, what was left of her dreams, and found herself living on the East Coast. They moved in with her brother, who hit his kids and urged his sister to do the same.

Six months later, they were living on Long Island. By the time Dan was eighteen, his mother had cirrhosis of the liver. All the nights working as a waitress and then allowing the men to buy her drinks and woo her to their beds had taken a toll on her life. It ended when Dan was a junior in college. The last he ever saw of his family was at his mother's funeral twelve years before. Dan sighed heavily at the thoughts of his family.

"It sounds like you have a fine family. Do you have any kids?" Dan said.

John and Aretha looked at each other with a quick glance. Dan knew that he'd asked the wrong question.

"We can't have any children." John looked

down at his right hand. "I've been injured and can't have children." He looked at his watch. The thunder was barely audible. "A distant family member passed on recently and we might adopt her two children. I don't know if we can legally because we're so poor. We'll see."

Dan wanted to ask what had happened to John, but had opted not to so that he wouldn't be asking two dumb questions in a row.

John looked at his watch again. "Well, I think the electricity might be on by now. What do you say we go to the Vanguards' and watch the Olympics?"

Dan hadn't been an avid Olympic observer. He remembered some of the greater Olympic moments, but could never recall watching much of the Olympics himself.

"I think I should get my bag out of the car and change." He stood up and pointed at his still wet, muddy shirt.

"Of course, how thoughtless of me. Do you need help?"

"No, it's one bag. I can get it." Dan got his bag and entered the kitchen again.

Aretha showed him to the bathroom and he decided to shave, considering he hadn't done that in nearly two days. Fifteen minutes later, he was dressed in a pair of shorts, a polo shirt, and sandals.

As they walked down the block, Dan's sandals became encased with mud. The television was already on and two other families were already seated in front of the television. The female gymnastics team was performing its first routines, and the families were talking about them. Dan recognized the Vanguards, Freemans, and Jeffries. There were ten people sitting in front of the television, half were white and half were black. Dan had several friends who were African-American, but he had never seen such equilibrium before. He knew this town was unique. These people helped each other. He had weathered the storm of his depression. He was ready to learn what love was.

Chapter 7

Dan went home with his adopted family at the end of the first part of the evening's Olympic broadcast. The American gymnasts had performed brilliantly, finishing second in the first component of the team competition. Dan became enamored with the beauty of gymnastics. He was looking forward to watching the Olympics again the next evening and had even begun to secretly hope that he would see some wrestling and baseball. Every adult in the room twisted, turned, and grimaced for the few seconds the gymnasts hung in the air to complete the various routines. The little gymnast, the star, barely in her teens, captivated the ten people in the room. The only one who looked mildly bored was Tarsi.

The ground was slow to absorb the rain water because of the high clay content. As Dan and the Freemans walked up the dirt driveway, Dan took off his sandals and walked barefoot the rest of the way.

"Would you like a piece of peach pie, Dan?" Aretha said.

"Yes, I think I would."

Normally, Dan would have a late night cup of coffee, but the evening hadn't become cool. In fact, it had become more humid as the evening wore on. He settled for a small glass of milk and a piece of the mouth watering peach pie.

Aretha yawned and excused herself for bed, and Dan decided he wouldn't be rude and ask for another piece.

"Aretha has to get up in the morning and cook breakfast for the workers. We'll probably have the same eight or nine people tomorrow," John said.

"How many people do you have in your congregation?" Dan said.

"We have about ninety-eight parishioners."

"The thing I don't understand, Reverend..."

"Please call me John."

"Sorry. The thing I don't understand is, who'd want to burn down a church, especially an integrated one?"

"Our parish tries not to dwell on that issue. I mean, we wouldn't want to feed into part of the reason why this was done. People who hate want us to think about them. They want us to hate just like them. They want to send us a message that to integrate, whether it be in a church or a restaurant, is not all right with them. They want us to hate them for burning down our church, and we won't do that."

John looked down at his hands, then turned over his scarred hand and looked at it more closely.

"Are you a religious man?"

Dan straightened at the question.

"I don't mean that as an inquisition. I'm not prying into your life, but there must be some reason why you came down to help, especially since this is a church."

"Well, I'm not your denomination. I'm a Roman Catholic," Dan said. "I haven't been in church much. When I was a child, I don't think I ever went in a church after I received confirmation. My mother didn't push religion; she was too busy pushing the liquor down her throat, and my father left us long before that. As I got older, I never really thought of church one way or the other. I didn't really think about it. I didn't blame God for my life as a child. I didn't think He hated me. I never even thought I had a bad life. I was good in school, I was good at sports, I was popular, and I was healthy. Somewhere along the way I saw that all of my accomplishments I did on my own." Dan smiled. "I hope that didn't sound like a confession or anything."

John returned his smile. "You and I are different, yet we are at the same place. The only difference is that I believe God has brought me here. I believe God brought you here as well. This is where we differ in philosophy. I believe that reporter wrote that article and got it published in your hometown newspaper. Your life is a shambles, you saw it, and something inside you was moved by it. If you came down here, you would have all the answers to change all that. What possessed you to read that article on that day? Why did the editor put that article in the paper that day? Why did you come here to rebuild a church? I'm not here to convert you, or bring you back to God. You never left God. He's been missing in your life for all these years, buried somewhere in your subconscious, and now the foundation on which you judge your life has been shaken by something and you can't figure it out. God has led you to a place where you can."

Dan sat in silence for a moment. Then he got up from the table. "I appreciate your thoughts on this, but I got in my car, I drove down here, I did all these things. No, I'm not sure why, or what answers I hope to get, but I know that God is something that's intangible and something that can't help me find this road I seek."

John stood with him. "Forgive me, friend. Like I said, we're both in the same place, and we have two different ideas on how this came to be."

"Well, what do you think is the reason for us being here at the same time?" Dan moved into the den and began setting up the couch for bed.

"I'll tell you a story, and you can decide whatever you want. When I was a boy, segregation in this country had been illegal for years, but most of the South still had problems adjusting. For the most part, this town had ended segregation long before the courts told us we had to. We're a small community, but we believe in God very strongly, and we've always maintained that there's no separation between races. Some of us believe that's why the railroad built an alternate route and stopped coming here. We believe that every time that train stopped in our town, the people on it saw the hate they held, and they knew it was wrong. Now, we were not interested in being the state or the country's savior. For one thing, we're so small, and the hate was so large. We saw on our televisions at night the hate, the fear, the prejudice, and we shook our heads in sadness. Millions of people quoted from the Bible and beat and turned hoses on black men and women because to them, the Bible said it was all right to hate. Deep down inside they knew they were using religion as a security blanket for their hatred.

"As a child, I somehow knew all of this because of what I saw my elders do all the time. My elders taught me right from wrong. My family was one of the wealthier ones in our community. My father was a caterer in the next town over. I had aspirations of taking over the business, being the only child in our family. I spent every spare hour working for him. In the fall of 1967, I was fifteen years old and starting a new year of school. Our community was much larger than it is today, but it was still small enough that we had to be bussed into the neighboring town thirty miles away to go to school. I guess I was a little naive because I interacted with white children in my own town.

"After the first week of school, the math class I was taking caught on to the fact that I was the brightest in class. There was this beautiful girl, a true angel, blonde hair made up in sausage curls, blue eyes, and creamy skin." John paused. His eyes glazed over. "She was having problems with the work. You could tell. She'd frown and wince whenever she was asked a question and I could tell by her dejected face that she was failing. One day I walked out of the classroom near her. I raised my arm to squirm past a fellow student and caught up with her down the hallway. I asked her where she was heading, and it turned out that she was heading toward the same part of the school I was. I asked her if she minded if I walked with her. I didn't notice at the time, but I guess she was a bit uneasy about it.

"I told her that if she wanted to, I could

help her understand the math class. It wouldn't have been a problem because my school bus arrived almost an hour early because the same bus picked up the neighborhood kids as well. If she wanted to meet in the library before school, I could help her prepare for the next test. She seemed to like the idea very much, and we set the time up for the next day to begin the tutoring session.

"Just then, a big older student with a varsity jacket put his arm around her.

"What are you doing with this nigger?" he said.

I was not bristled by the comment because in the South, even though you get bothered by a lot of bad things done to you, you learn to leave them alone."

"He was just offering to help me in that math class," she said.

"Ain't no nigger smart in math, and don't let him tell you so. You just come over to my house, and I'll teach you math."

She protested. "Every time I come over, all you want to do is listen to music or talk to your friends. Besides, you failed Fritz's class last year."

"I saw it then, but once again it was one of those things you don't realize until after the fact. The rage burned in his eyes just for a second. He was thoroughly embarrassed at having his girlfriend imply that he wasn't as smart as an underclass black boy. She must've seen it though because she looked me right in the eye and said, 'I don't think I'll be needing the help. Jimmy is real good in math and he can help me.' I just shrugged. What did I care if she flunked or not? I went to my next class and thought nothing of it.

"By the time lunch came, my friends had heard what I did and they were concerned for me. There was talk of the Klan going after me.

"The rest of the day went by and I didn't really worry about it all that much. I figured it was just talk because you hear that kind of thing all the time. Since the Vietnam War started heating up, there weren't that many incidents of the Klan in our area, anyway. I guess I was just plain ignorant back then, or just didn't want to believe that what I'd done, talking to a white girl, could elicit that much hate. I should've known better."

John brought over two glasses of local still whiskey and the two sipped on the hard liquor. The soft features of the night before had vanished and a mask of pain replaced it.

"I wasn't even looking. I had my head down thinking of that hot, dusty ride back to our town. I could see the yellow bus in the bright afternoon sun. I could see our bus driver, Mrs. Apletcn, with her hand on the door handle. I smiled, but on this day she didn't smile back. Suddenly, I lost sight of the bus altogether. I was hauled roughly away from the bus. I turned my head and saw Mrs. Apleton close the bus door. I saw it pull away, and I saw my friends screaming out the window, then looking up front and screaming at Mrs. Apleton. Everything was going so slowly. I remember so clearly turning my head in one direction, then another. All of the students around me were just walking, not looking in my direction, walking to their homes as if nothing was happening.

"I looked behind me at who was holding my hands and I could see the robes. I tried to break free then. I struggled wildly and screamed for help. The group moved faster and a man held me while he jogged with the rest of them. He lifted his hand and brought a billy club smack down on my forehead. I saw stars. By the time I was able to regain some aspect of my senses, a car trunk had been opened and I was dumped in the trunk. It was a long drive and I was scared. I didn't know where we were going, and I thought for sure I was going to die. I was just hoping that someone would tell my parents and they'd go to the police. I also hoped that my death would be quick and painless. I figured we were going somewhere and I was going to hang. Between the fear and the heat of the trunk, I began to sweat madly. I figured we were on Highway

Seven because it was the quickest and straightest road around and we'd hardly turned. I fell in and out of consciousness a few times because of the bumps in the road.

Anyway, we must have driven on a while because it was dusk when they pulled me out of the car. They dragged me and kicked me into a wooded area a short distance from the car, and we walked through there a little while. I remember looking up and seeing a hawk fly over head. I remember this hawk because it was the only thing in the sky. There were no clouds; the sun had dipped below the horizon, and the stars hadn't come out yet. After we'd gone a little ways into the woods, we came across a clearing that was encircled by the trees. In the center of the open area was a tree trunk sticking out of the ground and twigs and branches clinging all around it.

'We're going to burn us some dark meat,' the Klansmen yelled.

"They were all drinking, laughing, and calling me names, but I wouldn't waiver. They wanted me to fear them, to feel their power, and I wouldn't do it. I figured if I was going to die, I was going to die with pride. The pain from the ropes tore through me, but I kept it at bay because I concentrated on the hawk that sat perched on the tree. I just stared at it, wondered what it was like to be that hawk, wondered what it would be like to fly. I noticed as the darkness began to settle on the edges of the woods that the tree trunk was burned black. I was not the first person who was going to die here, and I was sure I wasn't going to be the last. They spit at me, and that was really the only way they broke my concentration on the bird. I looked back and saw that it had disappeared. I looked around for it but couldn't find it anywhere in the sky. It had simply disappeared. I felt as if I'd been abandoned and I screamed out in frustration. This was the first time I'd said or done anything since they got me in the car, so I guess they thought they were getting to me. They drank some more and taunted me more. Finally, the Klansmen got up off the log that was on the side of the center tree trunk. They drank some more and tied me up to the trunk. I could smell the remains of the previous fires. The most incredible thing happened just then. As two of them were tying me up, a third member brought out hot dogs and put them on a branch. It was the most inhumane thing I'd ever seen in all my years of living. They were going to barbecue some hot dogs while I burned to death. There wasn't a doubt in my mind that I was going to die in a few moments. I looked up and saw some stars, smelled the wildflower in the early evening dew. I was ready to die.

"They had torches lit, and one of the high school kids didn't look like he was having much fun anymore. He looked real worried. This didn't help me think that I was going to survive. I figured that he was in because he thought all they were going to do was scare me. He obviously hadn't run with the Klan much. I figured if he was worrying, then I was even more dead than I thought.

"They were arguing, but by then they had all been drinking heavily. A Klansman knocked a bottle over the kid's head. He was out cold, blood was oozing from a gash on his forehead. The other two moved toward me undaunted and lit the fire. I didn't really smell much at first, but soon I could smell the burning of leaves still attached to the branches. I looked out through the rising smoke and saw them admiring their work with the damn hot dogs in their hands. I wasn't afraid to die until right at that moment. I twisted, pulled, and tried to break free, but they just laughed even more. I felt pain then, right at my toes, then up my right leg. I looked down and saw that my pants were on fire. Then I smelled my own burning flesh. Mister, if there's one thing in life you ever want to avoid experiencing, it is the smell of burning flesh.

"I screamed and began to panic. They just sat there cooking their dogs and laughing. I could smell the cooked meat and watched them in grim fascination as they began to eat the hot dogs. I looked up once more at the sky and saw the outline of the hawk. I closed my eyes, heard a mighty crack, and dove into the confines of unconciousness that was waiting mercifully for me."

It was nearly two o'clock in the morning when John finished his story. They'd finished their third glass of whiskey. There were tears on John's cheeks, and Dan kept on wiping his own face. He knew he wasn't a prejudiced man, but he wasn't exactly perfect either. He had only one minority friend, and he had never really felt anything for the plight of the African-American. Now he understood because he was given one man's reality. He was given a man's fear at night. It wrapped around him, became his fears, his anxieties, his reality. The story provoked a feeling in Dan and he didn't know what it was.

John downed the rest of the whiskey. "I still don't know exactly what happened to this day. The sheriff came out after us when my friends told him what happened. He saw the car on the side of the road.

"How did he find you then? Blind luck?"

"No, the hawk."

"The hawk?"

"He was walking north, which is to say he was walking away from us. He heard the screech of the hawk and turned and saw it circling above the wood line. Then he heard my first scream and ran into the woods."

"The loud crack?"

"His gun. He shot and killed the Klansman."

John got up from the chair. "You look around here in town. We just have our faith. I told you that story because it brought me closer to God."

"How?"

John smiled. "A story for another time, perhaps. I told you this story to also illustrate something about this town and the South. The perception of the South is a lot like the story I told you. It's true that what happened to me, happened to many people who didn't live to tell anyone their own story, but that's not all the South is about. In a lot of ways the South is like this town. Sure there's hatred in this town, there's bigotry, and there's prejudice. You show me any town in America that doesn't have that. But we also have love for each other, we care for each other, and we help each other. This church burning was done out of hatred, but it's love that allows it to rise again. You're now a part of that process. Your work today and in the future will ensure that. You are a great man, Dan Meridian, you just don't know it yet!"

"And you do?"

"Look at our community. This town is poor and we have nothing, but we represent another part of the South. We love our neighbors as much as we love ourselves. That's what God has taught us. For as many people as try to tell us that it's God's book that teaches us to hate one another, there are a dozen more who tell us that the Bible teaches us to love one another. This is a community spirit that knows no racial boundaries.

"I told you that story tonight not because I was like so many of my fellow black men of the South, but because there was a white man, a man with a badge, who came to my rescue. In order to save my life, a black boy he never knew, he had to kill his best friend."

John allowed the words to float, resonate in the room and turn to silence. Then he walked across the wood floor. "We have a long day tomorrow. I hope we'll be able to make it."

Dan pulled the old sheet up his body, and though the summer evening was very warm and humid, he pulled the sheets way up over his shoulders and shook until he was able to fall asleep.

Chapter 8

Even though Dan hadn't slept more than five hours, he didn't feel that tired. He felt awake and alive. He'd gained a piece of the puzzle, and he knew that this was the place where he'd be able to find himself.

Like John had told him at night, the ground opened by the digging had allowed them to build the cinder block base, but it had also left gaping wounds in the clay earth, and tan puddles filled the holes causing more back breaking work.

There were many more workers than there were the previous day. Some only stayed for half a day. Most of the people were citizens of the town. They formed a bucket line, and by early afternoon the water was out of the ditches and they'd begun to build again.

By five o'clock most of the workers, their clothes drenched in sweat, pulled their way out of the pits and toward their homes. Some stayed and ate the barbecued ribs. Dan had no place to go, so he was at the table eating ribs with the rest of the people who stayed.

Not long after they'd finished eating, Dan once again struck up a conversation with Matt from Kansas City. "I think I learned something about why I'm here. I can't explain it exactly, but I feel as if I'm learning something about myself. It's almost as if the people here are teaching me something, but I haven't quite placed my finger on it yet."

"I think you see the incredible faith they have in themselves, which is in direct proportion to the faith they have in God," Matt said. "They simply live very happily with what they have because they have incredible faith in God, and all things come to be in His eyes."

"Are you a religious man?" Dan said.

"Well, I believe in God. That's why I'm here. Aren't you with God?"

"I believe in a God, Matt. I believe He's here. But I believe that each individual controls his life. You make the decisions as to what direction you want your life to move in. God doesn't have anything to do with it, but then again, I'm not sure about God much these days. I haven't been to Mass in a long time." Dan took a long sip of lemonade. He looked out to the field beyond the church. "That is a nice wide open field. Does the church own it?"

"I'm not sure," Matt said.

"If it does, I bet you can fit a baseball diamond out there. Left field might be a little short. Some balls hit might bounce up against the church, but I bet it'd be a fine baseball field. It certainly is flat enough."

"Are you a big baseball fan?" Matt said.

"I sure am. I coach it now and played the game for a long time when I was younger. I had an opportunity to try out with a major league baseball team, but I opted for college instead." Dan looked up at the sky.

"I love baseball, too. I catch as many games in Kansas City as I can," Matt said.

"I have some mitts, bats, and balls in the trunk of my car. What do you say we throw the ball around a little tomorrow?"

"Sure, I'd love it," Matt said. "I have two mitts in my car as well."

"So it's settled then. After dinner tomorrow."

Dan talked some more with Matt and was introduced to another member of the church, J.W. McGrath. Mr. McGrath was able to get most of the machinery needed for the first portion of the church from a company he worked for in the neighboring town. It was one of the many donations the surrounding communities gave the church to rebuild.

J.W. McGrath had a booming voice. "Tomorrow we should finish the basement portion of the church and fill in those holes that've been giving us headaches. We still need a lot of supplies, and if we don't get them soon, we'll have to stop building."

Reverend Freeman sat down and spoke to Dan and Mr. McGrath.

"I went to Gadsden today and checked up on our grant. We should be able to get that low-interest relief loan the government is sponsoring. I think we could have some money shortly."

"How much money are you applying for?" Dan said.

"Fifty thousand dollars."

"Fifty thousand dollars! That won't get the job done," McGrath said.

"It's all we can hope for," John said. We'll just have to hope to get the materials we need some other way." He sighed and got up. "Oh, by the way, don't forget tomorrow night the gymnastics team goes for the gold. We're going to the Vanguards' house to watch it if any of you gentlemen would like to join us."

Dan smiled. "I can't believe how interested in the Olympics everyone is around here. I spent last night watching the broadcast with about ten other people."

J.W. laughed. "You think that was a lot,

you should've been here for the opening ceremonies. Half the town saw it down at Susie's."

"Susie's?"

"The soda fountain restaurant."

"We take a lot of pride in our country and in the dedication the athletes have to competing," McGrath said. "We see it very much like the faith of God."

"Why is that?"

"Because you're given an ability by God, but you're not guaranteed to perfect that ability. What makes these athletes great is the way they overcome the barriers strewn in their path to get where they are. They sacrificed many things to get to that one moment in time. Their sacrifices are symbolic to the ones made in this town. For them, there are many temptations, drugs, cheating, losing motivation toward what seems like an impossible goal. We go through those same trials with them. We're constantly tempted and sometimes we lose our motivation to reach what seems like an impossible goal."

"What is the goal?" Dan said.

"Why, the goal is salvation, redemption, heaven. Those athletes are a mirror image of what we go through every day of our lives. It humbles them, it breaks them, but for those people, it leads them to the path of triumph."

Dan sat for a long time staring at his empty lemonade cup. He turned and looked at the church in its beginning stages and the charred remains behind it. He felt a sudden chill even though the temperature was still in the high eighties. He'd received two more pieces to his puzzle. He didn't know how many more pieces he'd need to complete the picture. He felt scared suddenly at the realization that he might never reach his goal of finding out why he came to this place. Lack of funds might prevent the completion of the church that somehow seemed to represent his own progression to this goal. He wanted to help, but he was only a teacher and his salary barely covered his family. He thought about this for a moment. There were many instances when he would work on odd jobs in order to keep food on the table.

He didn't know the answer to his life's journey yet. He was angered at the prospect that the journey might end before he truly understood the answers to the questions that were so important to his spiritual survival. Despite all of the greatness that he saw around him, he didn't understand how faith brought it to them. He overcame his difficulties with no help, not from God, not from his parents, not from his wife. He did it all, he did it without complaint, and he did it without gratitude. He found two pieces of the puzzle, and it led him toward a selfless path. He shook his head, confused, and found that the truck was nearly loaded. The sun had dipped below the tree line, but its orange glow still lit up most of the sky.

Dan pulled his baseball equipment out of the back of the pickup truck. He moved toward the open space. He picked up some stones and began to hit them with his bat. His thoughts were interrupted by Tarsi. Dan turned toward Tarsi, who looked at him stoically. Dan figured out what Tarsi wanted and pulled another baseball mitt out of his bag. Dan and Tarsi began to toss the baseball to each other. At first neither spoke. Then Dan decided to find out more about this intriguing young man.

"So, what do you like to do?" Dan said.

"I love to play sports. I love baseball."

"Do you play in school?"

"I'm going to play this year. I couldn't play any sports last year because my mom's health was failing."

They took a few steps back and threw the ball harder. Dan could see that Tarsi was strong and very athletic.

"Do you have many friends in town?"

"No, there aren't many teenagers in town. Most of my friends live closer to school."

"How far is the school from here?"

"The school is about forty-five minutes away."

The last rays of amber light started to fade and it was getting difficult to see the baseball. Dan collected the equipment, put it back in his bag, and sat on a bench next to Tarsi.

"Why did you come here?" Tarsi said.

Dan couldn't answer at first. "I don't know. I almost didn't come. Something seemed to draw me here. No matter how many times I thought about going home, I still seemed to always continue my journey."

"You were led here," Tarsi said.

"What?"

"You were led here. Something brought you here for a reason."

"You sound just like Reverend Freeman."

Tarsi smiled. "Thanks for the compliment."

"He seems to think the same thing about my arrival."

"I'm just going by what you've just said. You said something kept pushing you here. What do you think it was?"

Dan had a far off look as he spoke. "I wish I knew."

He got up off the bench and moved toward the truck that was already loaded.

"Sorry, I wish I could've helped you put everything away," Dan said.

John Freeman smiled upon him. "You were deep in thought, and Aretha and I both thought it'd be best to leave you be. You're a deeply troubled man, and I wish there was some way we could help you."

Dan looked at him. "You already have."

The truck rumbled and bumped along the road toward their home. Nobody said a word the rest of the way.

Chapter 9
"If the foundations are destroyed, what can the righteous do?" (Ps. 11:3.)

That night, Dan began to feel the exhaustion of the trip and the work. He went to work late the next day and felt completely invigorated as he played catch with a couple of townspeople and his new friend Matt. They'd been able to finish the basement portion of the structure and they filled in the mounds of dirt into the open pits. The workers were larger in force, more than double the number the previous two days. There seemed to be a sense of excitement and relief as the dirt got packed down against the cinder block.

It was a very important day. The town was abuzz with Olympic news, plans were set up for groups of townsfolk to watch the gymnastics finals at various homes, and with the state still in the midst of storm season, the covering of the great holes at the construction site meant a lot less cleaning up every morning.

The sun set just above the tree line in the late afternoon. The ball would sometimes get lost in the sun, but Dan always managed to pick up its path and catch it with plenty of time to spare. His eyes would keep tracking the ball without actually seeing it, a technique he taught his younger kids. He knew they would have to master that tip if they were ever going to get any further in understanding the complexities of the game. Dan felt great. He hadn't played any sports for months. His body ached, but he felt it begin to get stronger. He'd stopped working out because of his depression, but it felt good running for the ball and taking in huge quantities of clean Alabama air.

Dusk forced the group to bring the baseball mitts and balls back to Dan's car and deposit them in his trunk. He drove the short distance back to the Freemans' home where John was sitting out in the yard smoking a pipe. Dan had his windows open and smelled the sweet tobacco as he pulled up the driveway.

"Did you have fun?" John said.

"Sure. I had a great time."

"I could tell."

"How?

"You're less than a mile from here. I heard your cries of laughter. Noise travels over great distances when there isn't anything to compete with it."

"Oh, sorry."

"No need. We all got enjoyment out of it."

"How's that?"

"When you first arrived, you were the most serious thing I'd ever met. You had the look of a man with the weight of the world on his shoulders, but now you smile, and for just a few moments today, you looked very happy, and you've only been in God's country for three days."

Dan blushed, "I have to admit, I feel better than I have in months."

"Why is that?" John said, taking a slow drag from his pipe.

"I don't know. I just feel better."

"You have much to learn yet about yourself. You feel better, but you don't know why. You're only halfway toward recovery then. To be fully aware of yourself, to know why you act and feel the way you do, is something only a few individuals can do, but for you this must be done in order to save whatever it is you're trying to save. To finish with any less is a defeat."

"How do you know so much about life, about feeling?"

John laughed. "Believe me, I don't, just ask my wife. I know about you because I've seen many people just like you in my life. Some of them come to the inevitable conclusion, and some of them never make the entire journey."

"Will I make the entire journey?" Dan listened to his question and thought it sounded insane. He knew John less than a week and suddenly he found himself clinging to his every word. John pulled the pipe out of his mouth and looked up at the stars. "I cannot answer the question. I only know what conclusion you'll come to when you have completed the journey."

"What will that be? Dan asked doubtfully.

John laughed again. "If I told you, then the journey would be too easy, or you may not want to do it at all."

Dan sank a bit.

John got up and pulled the lawn chair off the ground. He was heading for the garage and stopped to look at Dan. "If I were you, I'd come in soon. As soon as the aroma of my pipe dies out, the mosquitoes will eat you alive."

Dan jogged up to John. They went in through the garage and Aretha had two pieces of peach pie waiting for them. Like giddy school children, they ate the pie and drank the glasses of milk beside it.

"You ask me about how I know so much," John said. "If you want to meet somebody who is a true master, talk to my wife. She knows everything about people."

Dan looked at Aretha across the kitchen table. "Well, what about me?"

Aretha smiled. "John's just teasing. I know

as much about people as the next person. All I know is that when someone's feeling good about himself, it's because he feels he is doing the right thing. The person likes this feeling; it's his security blanket. He wants to be in this place and strives to be in this place all of the time. I also know when people aren't happy, they aren't happy because they're doing something they do not feel is right. Even though their mind tells them it's all right, their heart tells them it's wrong. There's a great tug of war going on within their souls."

Aretha smiled and removed the empty dishes and glasses from the table and returned shortly with a mason jar of whiskey and two small glasses.

John smiled. "You see, the woman never fails to understand me." He poured two glasses.

Aretha called from the bedroom. "You better get ready, we're already late for the Olympics. We should be going soon."

John finished the whiskey. There was a twinkle in his eye. "You see what I mean?"

Ten minutes later, they were in a different home to watch the Olympics. There were two dozen people in a huge Victorian mansion. It was once likely a splendid sight, but was now in disrepair. Within ten years, the foliage would erase all signs that a house was even on the site.

The television was wider and almost brand new. The crowd of people marveled at the remote control with the split screen capability. When they arrived, the United States gymnasts were heading into their third event. There was a tremendous amount of excitement from both the audience on screen and the audience in the room.

"The U.S. just pulled into first place," Mrs. Pellitier said as she set finger food in front of the guests. "Help yourselves."

Dan decided to skip the food, but graciously accepted a cold iced tea.

As the American gymnasts moved to the horse for their final routine, the gold medal seemed to be theirs for the taking. There was a lot of excitement in the room. The U.S. women gymnasts, and their seemingly impossible dream of obtaining a team gold, seemed to personify the people of Spleen. Dan knew that for the gymnasts their goal was something unparalleled in U.S. Olympic history. For the people in the room, it was the completion of their church, and the promise that when that completion came about, the church would stand as a symbol that love conquers hate. Though the world focused on the athletic achievement before them, the group of about two dozen people focused on the courage the athletes displayed, and the faith they had in their abilities. It was the faith it would take in those athletes, the faith they had in themselves and their hearts that made a seemingly spiritual and physical connection with the town. It was a faith that surmounts even pain and the dark side of failure.

Each person, even Tarsi, had watery eyes as they were witnessing the redemption of the long-suffering gymnasts. The incredible faith they must have had to overcome injuries, history, doubters, and the competition. Yes, the members of that group felt much like the American gymnasts because they too needed to overcome the injuries of history, doubters, and lack of money to succeed at their goal. Though no one spoke of this, it was on everyone's mind. The Americans' biggest talent, a little princess of a girl, stepped up to the final event.

The announcers could be heard with the edge of excitement in their voices. "This is it. Team USA needs a little better than a nine to clinch the gold for the U.S."

Her success seemed certain. The celebrations had already begun in the arena as she took her run, her leap, her jump, her twists, her fall. Like a lost lamb in the fields, she stared dumbfoundedly on the mat, a place she shouldn't have been. She picked herself up gingerly, and suddenly she looked like what she was supposed to look like, a small, American girl at the age of fourteen. The arena seemed to overwhelm her, and she looked like a shadow of her former self. The group in the room watched with the rest of America as the little girl walked back to the starting spot, but like the rest of America, the group from the town of Spleen saw the noticeable change in her demeanor. She was no longer sure of herself. The camera panned to the American team as they gave this fragile child the thumbs up sign. It was almost as if it was the sign that faith was still with the team, still pulling for her.

The gymnast nodded her head, took a deep breath, listened intently to some encouraging words from her coach, and faced the judges. This little girl, the weight of a nation on her shoulders and needing a nine-point-six to clinch a medal, ran with a leap. The television camera panned to a close up of the gymnast's face. Dan could see the fire to compete back in her eyes, transformed in front of a nation. He watched as she leapt, bounced up, twisted, legs slightly apart, and began to land. She fell again! The little group from Spleen gasped in unison. When the score went up, tears flowed down the girl's cheeks. Dan felt the air in the room get sucked out like a punch in the stomach. He asked himself the frightening questions. Could it have been too much to ask for? Could all the hopes of one town, the very center of their faith, be reaffirmed and rest on the shoulders of a tiny fourteen year old child? Had they done what other people do and trusted the frailest of things to pin their hopes on? Did they dare to dream such lofty dreams, to believe in the faith so strongly that by personifying the achievements of the gymnasts, put their goal of rebuilding their church in jeopardy? Would they become like most over-achievers, so close, yet not quite there?

Dan began to hope as well. In only three days, he'd managed to come so far. His muscles ached from all the work. He'd seen himself in the dreams and faith of these gymnasts. Now the faith he was discovering within him seemed to melt right before his eyes, like a fierce nightmare in the coming dawn.

The announcers came back, seemingly recovered from the emotional drama of the two falls. The Americans still had one more vault, one more chance. The lowest score would be thrown out. Now it was up to the final gymnast, a veteran. The gymnast wet her lips, the pressure clearly recognizable in her eyes.

"Team USA needs a nine-point-six to win the gold medal," the announcer said.

The pressure seemed unbearable. No one seemed to breath as she raised her hand, darted toward the vault, the mask of competition firmly on her face. She ran, then flew through the air, twisted and turned, and crashed to the ground in a heap as she missed her landing. The entire audience gasped. The veteran gymnast, still on the mat, grimaced in pain. Like a dove with a broken leg, she limped back to the starting point. Pain, not despair, was on her face.

The television captured the fear, the anxiety, and the pain of the seemingly certain failure ahead. She showed her pain to a nation and it gripped it just as the other Olympians had. Her coach begged and pleaded. She seemed to draw on his strength and on her teammates' strength. Despite the pain, the fear, the possibility that to continue on would jepordize her chances in competing individually for a medal, she picked herself up.

Still limping, she approached the starting point, wiped her hands on her leotard, raised one hand, and began to sprint down the runway. With every step she took the pain could be seen on her ashen face. With wobbling certainty, she jumped on the ramp, pushed herself in the air, twirled with the greatest of ease, and stuck her landing on one incredibly strong leg.

The entire room erupted with the understanding of what this young woman had done. The Americans did it! They had overcome the odds; they'd fought adversity with faith as their only weapon. The gymnast, like the town of Spleen defied the odds. In the town of Spleen, the faith was restored, the will to achieve burned alive, and Dan saw it. He knew where it came from and longed to get to that place.

The moments that happened after the Olympic triumph of the gymnastics team were mixed forever with Olympic history. No machine on earth could measure the type of courage needed to overcome the odds. The injured gymnast had just proven to a nation that anything is possible, and the town of Spleen believed it .

As she collapsed in pain and begged for help, with the gold medal won by the Americans, and her place in the pantheon of Olympic heroes assured, the gymnast had given the town of Spleen the hope they needed. They'd rebuild the church. They'd find the money and resources.

The Olympic darlings all gathered on the stage for their medals. There they were for all the world to see. They were proof that when people band together, put aside their selfish desires, no matter what their race, ethnic background and circumstance is, anything... even the building of a church destroyed by hate, could rise up again through the only thing the town of Spleen had, hands of love.

Dan left the house in the middle of the celebration. He was just as amazed as the rest of the group, but the thrill left him empty inside. He began to walk up and down the street. He thought about his wife and children and his childhood. He'd been robbed of so many things early in life. Things only a family could give. Now he was acting like his father did, and he realized he faced something far greater than merely moving to something new and exciting. He wondered if his father was driven to the same crossroad. Dan felt the impulse to run then, to run away from Spleen, keep heading west, further away from the answers. He needed help but didn't know where to turn. He felt helpless. The sweat seeped through his shirt, and for a brief instant, the hatred for his father's leaving him no longer existed. He knew the fight or flight reaction his father, and perhaps his grandfather, fought with. Dan didn't know if his own battle was already lost. His heart sank in despair. The idea that he could end up like his father scared him. The desire to flee overwhelmed him. He knew as a child the pain of his father's leaving. Tears began to swell in his eyes because he saw his own two children, who'd never know their father again if he chose the wrong path to follow. Suddenly he smelled the tobacco of John's pipe.

"You're hurting tonight?"

Dan made no reply.

"I can tell. I knew right in that room when that gymnast stuck the landing in there. When she achieved the impossible, you stood straight up like someone had slapped you. You realized something in there and it frightened you. You came out here and tried to run away from it." John's voice was rising, almost as if he was angry with Dan.

"Are you running away? Something's eating inside you, something only you are going to have to deal with. It's something more than laying a few bricks. You have to see past the physical and get into the spiritual aspect of why you are here. It is not a physical journey you seek, Dan; it is a spiritual one. Are you ready to admit that now?"

Dan began to walk away, but John, full of anger, stepped in his way. The smoke from his pipe rose in unison with his heavier breathing.

"You know, maybe it's time to finish that story from the other night," John said. "I didn't know about my fate, or the fate of any of the other participants involved in my abduction that night, until much later."

Dan began to move away and John let him go.

"I didn't know because I was in the hospital. I was in a coma."

John raised his voice so that Dan could hear him from down the road. Dan stopped.

"I was in a coma for two weeks. They didn't even know if I was going to live. They gave me a transfusion, they performed skin grafts, and I was beginning to heal, but I didn't know it. I didn't want to know it because I could feel and hear in my coma, but I could not feel the pain or fear of what happened to me. I was in my own special place and I didn't want to leave. I ran away from my pain. Though it was a different kind of pain, it's no different than what you're doing with your life.

"Something changed all that, though. I heard

my name from a voice I'd never heard before. I turned and opened my eyes. In the doorway of the hospital room was a man I'd never seen before. A black man. What was interesting about this black man was a scar on the right hand side of his face and clothes I couldn't recognize. He interested me, so I decided to stay out of the darkness and hear what he had to say. He came in, sat down beside me real close so I could see his blood shot eyes and his scar.

"The stranger said, 'You're not going to understand any of this right now, but you will someday. You need to live so that you can help people. Someday you'll help somebody, and it'll be special because you will learn as well as he. There are a great many good things you will do, but you have to want to do them. You have to have your faith in yourself and in your God.

"He got up out of his seat. I didn't even have time to ask him his name. I remember wanting to, but he felt so familiar to me that I felt embarrassed because I felt I should know him. I wanted to move toward him, toward the light that shone just beyond him. I wanted to speak, but found that I could not. At the doorway, my parents came in. When they saw me, they were crying and happy because I was out of my coma and their prayers had been answered. After a few minutes, I asked my parents about the man who came to see me. The question really upset my father, I guess because he had seen my scar, and I wasn't aware I had one. He said there was nobody in the room when they came in. At that point I knew the visitor had been a message from God. From that day on I dedicated myself to making people feel the faith. It didn't take long for me to get over my physical deformity."

The pipe in John's mouth had long ago gone out. Dan could no longer smell the rich aroma, and it was like a spell was lifted off him. He began to walk away again.

"What's that got to do with me? How can that help me?" Dan said.

John smiled. "Because I forgot all about that episode in my life. It was the furthest thing from my mind, but Sunday night I had that same dream again, just exactly the way I did all those years ago. It scared me half to death. I went to the bathroom to wash my face and I looked into the mirror and saw the same blood shot eyes from my dream."

Dan raised his hand as if he had enough.

"Doubt it if you want, but I find the coincidences too revealing. The first time I had that dream in three decades, exactly the same, and the next day you drive up to our church and you need help."

Dan stopped in his tracks. He didn't know what to believe, but he didn't want to give John the satisfaction. He hesitated and continued his long walk.

How many hours he walked he didn't know. It was late when he finally came upon the Freemans' home. He didn't know how he wound up there. This was another unexplained event of the evening, but somehow through all of the meandering of the evening he'd managed to get back to his starting point. He pulled his keys out of his short pocket and opened his car door. Matt stepped out of the shadows.

"I spoke to John tonight. He was concerned about your well being so I thought you could use some company."

Dan started the car, "You want to go to a bar? I could use a drink and some sports scores."

Matt smiled, "Sounds great."

They drove west into the heart of a storm. It took nearly twice as long to get to the next town as it should have, but eventually the storm subsided and Dan could see a bit more of the road. They got to town and asked a gas station attendant where the nearest sports bar was. Dan noticed a mall in the background and made a mental note to visit the mall later.

"Center Field is two exits off the interstate west."

"Center Field? Sounds like the perfect place," Dan said.

"They call it Center Field because it's in the middle of a huge field. It's about five miles out of town. Still, they have a satellite dish, and they put four or five different events on a dozen screens."

"Sounds great!"

Ten minutes later they found Center Field. The bar was small, wooden, and green like a baseball outfield wall. A giant bat, baseball, and glove hung over the front. They sat down in a booth where they could see the Atlanta Braves baseball game. Dan enjoyed the Olympics, but he hadn't seen a baseball game in over a week.

He needed a lift. His spirits were down and he felt the perfect cure would be to see some baseball and reflect on the events of the past few days.

He and Matt didn't talk much since both were absorbed in every moment of the game. As the game progressed, they ordered more beer and some bar food. When the game was over, they watched ESPN's Sports Center and got caught up on all of the Olympic action as well as the highlights of other baseball games throughout the country.

Dan's spirits improved. He and Matt talked to each other as if they were old friends. Finally, as two o'clock approached and they realized they still had to drive forty miles back to Spleen, they asked the waitress for the check.

Dan took his keys out of his pocket and opened his car door. Suddenly, Matt decided he needed to use the bathroom, so Dan waited by the car while Matt went back inside.

Two men approached Dan. One wore a black Harley Davidson tee shirt, and the other a smudgy white tee shirt with an open flannel shirt. They didn't seem friendly.

"What are you doing all the way here from Maryland?" the man with the Harley Davidson shirt asked.

"Just helping out some people rebuild their church," Dan replied, hoping his mentioning his good deed would turn aside their anger.

Dan was no stranger to bar fights. He had been a bartender to support himself in school. He wasn't scared of the situation yet.

He could smell the alcohol on their breath and quickly sized up the two men. They looked pretty coherent. Dan estimated that they could hold their liquor well. He wasn't sure he even wanted to get involved in a fight in the middle of nowhere. He didn't know the law, he didn't know the area, and he didn't know how many friends these guys might have inside.

"Look, guys, I'm just a Southern boy from Maryland come down to God's country to see the beautiful land of Alabama for myself," Dan said. He laid down a slow Southern drawl.

It didn't matter much to the men from the bar. One of them belched loud and clear through the still, humid air. Dan quickly figured that the plan wasn't working. Dan tried to figure out his next move. He didn't have one.

He noticed they were edging closer to the car. His mind turned over the different possibilities and each outcome didn't have him coming out on top.

Matt suddenly moved up behind them, closer to the car. He was practically on top of the two men. They were so inebriated that they didn't know that he was there. Dan realized then that he overestimated their ability. He turned his attention to the keys in his hand. He shifted the keys so that the ignition key was held out away from the others.

Dan decided to stall for time. "Look guys, I came down here to help build a church. I came here to catch some scores because I'm a baseball fan. What I'm trying to say is, I was just passing through and I'm heading out. If you want to make an issue out of it, fine, but I'm really just looking to get on home now."

Dan took several steps toward his car door. He now needed only to jump in the car, close the door and start the car. The two men took three steps toward him, and Matt mimicked their approach.

"You're not going anywhere until we give you some of that real Southern hospitality," the heavy set one said.

The two men took two steps closer, and they were less than ten feet from Dan. Quick as lightning, Dan sprang into the car. He saw Matt out of the corner of his eye running toward the car.

The two men both went for Dan. They both got in each other's way, which allowed Dan to get in the car and close the door. Within a few seconds, Dan heard the door to the other side of the car open and lock. It took only a second for the engine to turn over. He heard a thumping and the car jerked up and down. The two men were kicking the back of his car.

He put the car in drive and slammed on the accelerator. The car sped out of the parking lot and toward the interstate, leaving a trail of wet clay and gravel. Dan pulled out onto the east bound interstate and eased off the gas only when he had nudged the car passed seventy miles per hour. He could see the lights of the mall parking lot in the distance. Barely a word was spoken.

In a few moments Dan sped passed the mall. He took a quick look in the rearview mirror, and as he'd suspected, a car's headlights bore down on them. He pushed down on the pedal and the car lurched an additional ten miles an hour. The nose of the car began to shake. It wasn't built for this speed.

Dan took a quick look into the mirror again. The headlights were closer but still a great distance behind. He'd passed the exit to the mall. He knew the next exit was still miles away. His mind tried to calculate if he had enough distance between his car and theirs to get to the next exit and maybe get to a public place. He looked in the mirror again and realized his greatest fear of the chase. The local men had a much faster car. He floored the accelerator and the car screamed in agony as it nudged close to ninety. He was losing control of the car, and he was a good thirty miles from Spleen, the only area he knew well enough to try to hide. There was no way he could trust where he was going on any of the other exits. Dan passed a sign with the names of towns and their distances. Dan thought it was odd that Spleen wasn't on the list.

The car was getting nearly impossible to control from the rain that was still on the street. The tires weren't new, either. The car bore down on them and was less than a quarter of a mile away. Dan estimated that within a few minutes at their current speed, the car would catch them.

Gently, Dan eased up on the accelerator. The car slowed down to a barely manageable eighty miles an hour. The car gradually got closer so Dan could see vaguely what type of car it was. He thought it looked like an old Mercury Cougar.

"What are you doing?" Matt said feverishly.

"Do you know where we can turn off safely?"

"No, I don't."

"I have a plan." Dan yelled above the roar of the engine.

"I sure hope so. We're dead men right now."

Dan drove on, trying not to let the odometer read lower than eighty. He wanted to slow down enough so that the car behind him could catch up, but he also wanted to still leave the impression that he was still trying to outrun them.

The car was less than one hundred yards away. He saw a hand in the passenger seat throw something out the window. It looked like a beer can. Dan smiled. With any luck the driver was drinking and his reaction time was slowing. He heard the roar of the other engine as it made its final push to catch up.

Dan took his eyes completely off the road and concentrated on the rearview mirror.

The driver didn't make a move around him. He was less than twenty feet from the car. Dan couldn't get a good read on the driver's speed, but he could plainly see that the driver intended to hit him from behind. Dan studied the driver intently and saw that the driver pulled more to the right than the left. That was the opening he needed. Dan hoped he kept the car's speed the same. He'd slowed it down to seventy, too fast for what he wanted to do, but it was better than eighty. He waited, and then when the car was less than ten feet from him, he swerved to the left and slammed on the brakes. The car behind him pulled right and zoomed past him. That was all Dan could see of the other car because his car pulled into a fishtail that sent it off in uncontrollable circles. Dan fought hard to stay on the road as his car slowed down. Dimly, he heard the car ahead of him apply its brakes.

Dan fought the steering wheel for control of the car. The little car sailed off the highway and onto the grass meridian that separated the east and west lanes. The car slowed down drastically when it hit the grass.

Dan still fought with the steering wheel and muttered through clenched teeth. "Come on God, give me this one. Help me out here."

The dirt was loose and slick from the rain, and although Dan swore the passenger side of the car lifted off the ground, the little car didn't flip. It slowed down enough so that Dan regained control of the car and steered it back onto the eastbound lanes. Quickly he checked the speedometer, and miraculously he was traveling at nearly thirty miles an hour when his car straightened out and moved eastbound down the highway. As he regained control of the vehicle, his eyes caught the other car, still spinning out of control on the other side of the road. It sailed into a ditch and abruptly stopped. The two men began to pull themselves out of the open windows. The car soon disappeared out of sight.

Ten minutes passed before either of them could speak.

"We almost got fried back there," Dan said.

"You're not kidding. I think those guys would've killed us."

"I think if they caught us on the highway, they would've killed us. I think they just wanted to put a scare into us some outside the bar."

"Well, you didn't help the situation when you spit up all that wet clay and gravel at them. You must've soaked them good!"

They started to laugh about it, but Dan's hands still shook.

It was odd for Dan. It seemed as if they'd just gotten off the ramp of the interstate. They made a few turns, maybe two or three miles off the interstate at most. Spleen was very close to the highway, but from all indications from the interstate, the town of Spleen didn't exist. Dan began to wonder if it did indeed exist. It was incredibly foggy in town. The storms did nothing to lift the oppressive humidity, and it took Dan two tries to find the house.

"Are you going to go to church with John and Aretha on Sunday?" Matt said.

"I don't know." Dan thought for a moment. "I can't remember the last time I was in a church."

"You have a lot to be thankful for, especially after tonight."

Dan thought about the evening, especially the moments when he was asking for God's help in steering the car to safety. He couldn't remember asking for God's help for anything before.

"I guess there are many things I should be thankful for. I'm not a very religious man, at least I didn't think I was," Dan said

Matt stepped out of the car and closed the door, then leaned in through the open window. "If you look at the people in this town and you see what little they have, you think surely God's not in these people's hearts. They don't have anything. They just have this incredible faith in God, and it seems to be enough for them. Yet we have it better in so many other ways and we don't have faith in God nearly as much as these people do. We're not thankful for what we have.

"Think about it. What do these people have to be thankful for? They have nothing. Yet they have such a profound grasp of faith in God that it boggles my mind. I guess it makes me want to be more committed to God. He turned to walk away.

"After tonight, I'm a little closer to being a true believer."

Dan pulled away and eased towards John's home.

"Me, too," he muttered.

He smiled at the irony, saw that a light was on inside the house, and entered through the garage. As he entered the living room, he saw that the bed was made up for him. The family was asleep, and he thought it'd be a good idea to go to sleep as well. They all had a long day ahead of them, and he knew now that he wanted to be a part of that day.

The thought of failure plagued his mind, and soon it was daylight. Dan watched as the animals around the home began to stir to life, each one awakening the other. After a short time, cars could be heard in the distance along with shouting voices. Soon afterward the house came to life. Dan didn't get any sleep that night, but he still managed to summon the strength to take a shower, down three cups of coffee, and go with John to the work site.

John wasn't himself this morning. Normally cheerful, he looked haggard as if he himself hadn't slept.

When they arrived at the work site, they immediately woke up, for they couldn't believe what their eyes saw. There were over sixty people standing around the site. Most of the workers didn't seem to notice John. Some waved, but John couldn't wave back.

"I haven't seen some of these people in months," John said, marveling.

John talked with a few of the workers who'd worked more frequently than the others. It was already ten o'clock, and the workers were eager to get started. John consulted with the construction chief, a congregation member named Stanley who was a retired engineer for the army. They quickly figured out what to do, and the workers were grouped into work crews. Some continued to build the brick wall, and they soon completed their job. Some groups were in charge of cutting the lumber and other groups began to put the pieces of lumber together. Before long, the work was underway with great excitement. John worked side by side with Dan, who was framing out sections of the church with a group of men.

"That's all anyone is talking about, the Olympics last night," John said eagerly. "I think our congregation has always sought this church as our goal, but some of us didn't believe it would come true, so they didn't come by as frequently as they wanted to. They have faith again."

"I thought you said most of your congregation was out of town working," Dan said.

"They are. These are their relatives, friends, neighbors. These are people from other towns. Now they're here, all of them from different backgrounds, different denominations, all working to build our church. They won't let us give up." Dan saw tears well in John's eyes, and he recognized for the first time how much this meant to him. Dan was exhausted. Every limb in his body screamed with pain and soreness. John looked haggard. Although the two were desperate for rest, they worked at a feverish pace. They rested in shifts for lunch so that work was done on a continual basis. They sat in the deep Southern heat of the afternoon, but none of them complained.

Even in the heat of the day, when limbs were too tired to move, they talked universally of the great courage of the Olympians. Though Dan was exhausted from work, his mind turned over the events of the past twenty-four hours. Each time it came to an inevitable conclusion, but he rejected it each time, not wanting to go down that road just yet. It began to get late, but the heat didn't give up.

Down the road to the church, a dust cloud began to form as a car approached. The car, shimmering in the summer light, stopped just short of the church driveway. Two officials in jeans and summer Oxford shirts with ties stepped out of the car. They put on hard hats, pulled briefcases out of the back seat of the car, and walked toward the work zone. John saw them and straightened up. Most of the workers kept on working.

"What is it?" Dan asked, concerned.

"It's Judgment Day," John murmured.

"What?"

John came out of his trance. "Oh, sorry. One person is the federal relief fund loan officer, and the other is the Gadsden loan officer who'll be in charge of our loan, if we get one."

John excused himself. Dan watched as John went to a water hose, washed his hands, and poured water over his head and neck. He then strode over to the two men with an air of confidence and shook their hands. They sat down at the table under the tent and a woman Dan didn't recognize provided each of them with a drink.

Dan turned away from them and began to work

again. When he looked up, John and the men were gone from their seats under the tent. When he turned to look for the car, he found that it was no longer there. Instantly, an alarm ran off in his mind and he looked for John. First, he looked for him by the tent, then by the watering hole, then in front of the street. Finally, he walked toward the remains of the church. Behind what remained of a wall, he found John praying on the floor.

Dan watched over John as the beating, setting sun pounded over John's exposed shoulders and arms. He could see the scar on his arm clearly. He saw how it ran all the way up his arm to his neck and up his face. Finally, John stood up, dusted the soot off his jeans, and looked at Dan.

"Thank you for waiting for me to finish," John said.

"No problem." Dan hesitated. "So? What's the news?"

John looked at him with the emotion of the moment written on his face.

"We'll be able to get a loan from the federal government to finish our church."

Dan brightened. "That's great. You must be very happy."

"Well, the bad news is that we're going to be off a bit."

"What do you mean?" Dan didn't understand.

"The government can't give us more than thirty thousand dollars. We needed at least fifty to complete the job. Somewhere along the line, we need to find twenty thousand dollars in order for the church to be completed."

John smiled. "It appears we still have one more vault left in us though. Let's go get something to eat by the tent. The workers will be happy for us. They have something to do for the next few weeks."

Dan and John left the ruins of the old church behind. The workers had dwindled to about twenty-five. Many workers had left to go home for the evening. Dan looked at John and saw that there was no doubt in his mind that the twenty thousand dollars needed would turn up somehow. Dan couldn't see what John pinned his hopes on, but it was there. Dan hoped he would learn the answer soon.

Chapter 10

The Olympic broadcast that night paled in comparison to the night before. Many of the people in the Van Ryans' living room were completely exhausted, and there wasn't nearly as much excitement and conversation as the night before. Dan and the Freemans excused themselves early, and by nine o'clock Dan was comfortably in bed. While awake, Dan wondered through the calmness of the evening about John's horribly torturous night years ago,and he was convinced that this was another sign sent by Him.

Dan woke up. When he was finally conscious enough to go to the bathroom, he realized that the house was very hot. His first inclination was that it was going to be hotter than usual. Upon checking his watch, he discovered that he not only overslept into the morning, but he overslept into the afternoon. He moved toward the kitchen and saw a note.

Dan:

"We went to the church site. Don't worry about working today. We will have a lot of people again, and you deserve a day off."

Dan was a little relieved that he wasn't going to work. He was sore and tired. He lay down on the bed and contemplated taking a shower. Before he knew it, he fell asleep for another hour. Finally he got out of bed, took a shower, and went into town to get a late lunch.

Getting to the town was easy. He was less than a mile from it. Soon he found himself at the soda fountain restaurant. He eventually consumed two floats, and they alone just about filled him up. While he was eating lunch, he read the paper. He had been out of sports news other than the Olympics for some time now, and he quickly caught up. Dan read more deeply into the issues affecting society. The drive by shootings, the senseless violence of the world around him seemed more painful and immediate to him now. He moved to the next section, the advertisements. He casually read the car and home sales. He browsed through the personals and jumped with a start. He reread the advertisement. It became another piece of the puzzle for him.

He jumped up to the counter. "Do you have a pay phone here?"

A woman in her forties, who looked like she could barely lift a finger from the heat, nodded toward the back. Dan ran to the phone. The paper expanded in the air and crumbled backward in a matted mess. He dialed the number and waited anxiously. A women with a raspy voice answered the phone.

"Good afternoon. My name is Dan Meridian. I'm responding to the advertisement in the paper. May I please speak to, uh, Father Amante Ricco?"

The receptionist left him on hold and it was several minutes before a man, who sounded like he'd been an authority figure much too long, answered.

"This is Father Ricco."

"My name is Dan Meridian, and, boy, am I glad I read your advertisement. Are they still for sale?"

"Yes, they are."

"Good. I'd like to talk to you about them. I'm in Spleen, Alabama..."

As Dan spoke to the man over the phone, he couldn't believe the sheer luck. To any observer, he looked like a kid enjoying his first Christmas.

Night came too slowly for Dan Meridian. He couldn't contain his excitement. He couldn't wait to tell John and Aretha the news. By the time he got to their house, however, they'd already gone out to watch the Olympics. They left a message for him, and he tore out of the house.

Before he knew it, he was at the VanRyan house, running up the porch steps and into the house. He was completely out of breath. The gathering was much smaller than the day before, but there were still about six people there again. It took a full minute for him to catch his breath.

Finally, still flush with excitement and breathing hard from his run, he began to tell them the great news he had.

"I'm eating at the soda fountain and I buy a paper at the newsstand across the street. I come across the advertising section. Normally, I don't even read the section, but for some reason I just decided to. Anyway, I see this advertisement. The Roman Catholic diocese in Hartford, Connecticut, is renovating churches. They have used pews for sale. I called up because they're selling church pews. I figure we need church pews right? Anyway, I talked to him for nearly half an hour." Dan stopped and realized something he hadn't before. He wasn't sure how the town would respond to this intrusion.

"How much will they cost?" John said.

"That's the beauty of it, John. They're free."

"Free?"

"I talked the Pastor into donating the pews to our church."

"Are you kidding me? We're getting pews for

free?"

"Yes, sir," Dan said excitedly.

"That's only the beginning. I called up a national moving company, explained our situation, and they're delivering them for free right here. They should be here in a week."

It was difficult for John to contain his excitment. Quickly, he pulled a notebook from his pocket.

"We should save about four thousand dollars."

The entire room gravitated toward Dan and slapped him on the back. It felt like he finally belonged to something, to a part of them.

"In addition to the church pews, members of the congregation called some area lumber supply companies in Gadsden. We didn't have any luck at first, but then we really hit pay dirt. Tomorrow we're going to get a shipment of two hundred pieces of one by four by eight for free, and I talked with a brick dealer. If we pay for half the brick work we need, they'll pay for the other half."

It was pure euphoria in the room, and Dan absorbed every bit of it. He'd finally learned to appreciate the feeling of doing something for someone else. He knew then that he was on the spiritual journey, and he was just beginning to enjoy the ride!

It was late in the evening, and it was John's turn to lie awake. He sat in the kitchen with

Dan and couldn't believe the turn of events. "The past forty-eight hours had been an incredible windfall," he said turning to the numbers on a pad and paper. He showed the numbers to Dan. Dan saw that he had saved the congregation a tremendous amount of money and he was delirious over his achievement.

"Between the money we have, and the generosity of so many others, I'm estimating that we could enclose the church, buy the drywall, and maybe get the electrical work done. The plumbing, floor work, ceiling, altar, and books are the high dollar items still out there. The congregation has already begun to cut some of the costs by finding cheaper alternatives. If I could just pick up six or eight thousand dollars more, we could get the church up and running at least. It would be functional, and the rest of the items could be bought a little at a time." John was breathless with anticipation. Suddenly, he snapped to attention as if an electric cable crackled through his body

"I've got an idea!" He rushed to the phone right then, but turned back to his chair when he realized that at three o'clock in the morning, nobody would be in the office. "I guess it will have to wait until morning," he said, resigning to get some sleep.

Dan moved toward his own bed, the excitment of the afternoon keeping him awake, he knew in the back of his mind that neither he nor John would be doing much sleeping that night.

He turned over on his side and looked out of the living room window. Though it was dark, he wasn't interested in what he could see. It was what he couldn't see yet that excited him because he realized that soon he would be able to see more than he ever had before.

Chapter 11

As dawn came to Spleen, John was already up pacing the floor. He had a series of phone calls to make. If he got the answer he needed with the first one, the rest would all fall into place. Unfortunately, the first phone call could not be made until nine in the morning. It was only ten after six.

Dan watched John's ordeal silently. Dan was exhausted from all of his work, and he logged in for another full day. It was Friday. Whatever work they could get done today would be it for the weekend. A town picnic was planned for Saturday, and services were ready for Sunday. Even though the town of Spleen had one of the highest unemployment rates and the lowest per capita income per family in the country, the citizens worked hard tending their own plots of land and bartering for what items they needed. The town survived completely on the will of the individuals, the faith they had in each other, and God watching above them.

Before long the rest of the household, as well as the rest of the town, were awake and preparing for the day. Dan took Aretha to the work site, and John went into town to make some phone calls. Dan was impressed with the amount of work completed in the day he wasn't there. The frames they made two days before had been completed and set up so the church reached toward the sky. Stilts supported the framing work to prevent it from falling over. Once again a large number of workers showed up. The reconstruction had become a huge project. Even though the number of people dwindled to about forty workers, it was still thought to be enough workers to finish the framework. When told that the frame work needed to be completed to decrease the chance of it falling in a storm, the workers wasted no time. By noon another section had been raised and secured. The workers broke for lunch in shifts and once again Dan sat next to Matt from Kansas City.

"Do you want to play some ball tonight?" Matt said.

"Sure," Dan replied. "You know I want to get

out of this town for a while. Do you want to go back to that mall we passed the other night? I thought I saw a sign for a sporting goods store. We could buy baseball equipment there."

Matt readily accepted. "There looked like there was a restaurant in the mall. I was thinking of eating dinner there one night."

"Sounds perfect."

As they were speaking, several large trucks entered with huge payloads. The four by eight pieces of plywood had arrived. The workers gave a big cheer as they were unloaded and placed near the old church. A stark contrast showed between the new tan colored wood and the burnt out pieces. The truck drivers were treated like heroes when they finished. The women made them huge lunches. Finally, the truckers left with a wave and a trail of dust.

The workers returned to their work with the goal of finishing the final piece of the framework. At around three-thirty in the afternoon, the final frame wall was raised, and by four o'clock it was secured. The past three days had been a whirlwind of emotion, and with the work they had in mind finally complete, many of the workers seemed to run out of gas.

As many of the workers were heading for their homes, a car rusted out on one side and dented on the other, screeched into the dirt driveway and stopped. John jumped out of the car before the engine had even turned off. He was waving several papers in his hands.

"I have great news!" he cried as he approached the group.

"I just got off the phone with Noland Incorporated, and they have finalized the plan."

"What plan?" A worker with an overgrown beard said.

"I called J.W. Watkins this morning."

"What did you want with him?" The same worker said with a bit of disgust in his voice.

"I asked him if he'd donate some of his time and put in the plumbing work for our church."

"You asked J.W. to do what?"

"Relax, Billy," John said.

"Why did you go and do that?"

"He's one of the best, one of the only, certified plumbers in the area, and since the code clearly states we need a licensed plumber and electrician to do that kind of work, I figured J.W. would be the best person for the job."

"Is that what you thought? You didn't run this by us?"

"What was there to tell you? If J.W. was going to do the work for free, then I saw no debate in the matter. Everyone here knows we're still over eight thousand dollars in debt. If we could save a thousand dollars having someone work on the plumbing, that'll help us reduce that debt. Besides, I thought it'd be nice if he'd come back to us."

Billy seemed to get more angry as the proposal continued.

"You really didn't think he'd come back to the church, especially our church. We all remember the way he left. He's gone bad and we all know it."

"Billy, he said yes."

There was a collective groan from the audience.

"You know what we believe in this congregation," John said. "If God can show mercy on his disciples, if he could show mercy to us, then we must live in His shadow and must have mercy on those who hurt us, especially when this is a clear indication that he wants to come back to God."

Billy shook his head in disbelief. "He's coming back to God?"

"I believe he will if we show him there are open arms here."

The workers all talked among themselves.

"We'll welcome him," Billy said resignedly.

John smiled. "Great. After I called him, I negotiated with Noland. They will donate the plumbing equipment if we buy the electrical equipment from them. I figure we are going to save another five hundred dollars."

For the third day in a row, a miracle happened.

That evening Dan and five other members of

the town participated in a small baseball game. As the sun settled on the horizon, a sweaty Dan placed the baseball gear in the trunk of his car. An idea suddenly came to him.

"How do you feel about buying a few more mitts and balls when we go to the mall on Saturday and getting a few teams up? We could outline some base paths."

"I think it's a great idea," Matt said. We should get some of the workers to help us out and dig out a real baseball diamond."

Plans were set in motion. They would begin work on Monday evening. Dan headed back to his adoptive home. There were no plans to watch the Olympics that night, mostly because of the big picnic that was set for the next day. Dan was once again exhausted from the day's work and had no problem falling to sleep early that evening. As Dan closed his eyes, he began to think of his family.

His dream that night was pretty simple. He was with his wife and two children and they were on a vacation somewhere. He couldn't see where, but he saw large mountains, maybe it was California. The place didn't matter much. It was the happiness that he felt that he remembered the most. When he awoke, he was happy. He saw this dream as another jigsaw puzzle piece. They were coming in rapid succession now. He'd been in the town for less than a week and already felt like he was halfway done with his journey.

He spent Saturday afternoon in the hot Alabama sun. Everyone who was still in town came to the picnic. Dan estimated that about one hundred and fifty people were there. Every family of the town brought a dish to contribute to the picnic. Three pit barbecues blazed with delights, a whole pig in one, a rack of beef in the other, and hot dogs and burgers in a third. Games of all varieties were played, especially horseshoes. A patchwork of tablecloths joined together huge tables.

The picnic could've been compared to a traditional harvest feast if not for the oppressive ninety-eight degree heat. The townspeople didn't seem to mind the temperature much, but Dan wasn't getting any closer to feeling comfortable in it. Dan saw something at the picnic he thought he'd never see. Despite all the hardships the town had endured, the intense poverty, the rebuilding of the church, the removal of many of their families to make ends meet, the town seemed thankful for what they had. For the life of him he couldn't think of much that they had. Dan sat under the shade of a tree near the massive open field that had become the picnic area for the day. He tried to become part of the town, to feel what they felt, but he couldn't. He sat alone under the tree, feeling every bit of his self-imposed exile.

Dan still hadn't figured out the reason why the townspeople could be so thankful after the decades of poverty they had endured. After dinner, the crowds began to disperse as thunder clapped in the distance.

Chapter 12

Dan awoke to the noise of John and Aretha scrambling to get ready for church. He'd only slept about four hours, but his mind was racing with the events from the previous evening. He pulled himself together, grabbed some leftover breakfast, and moved to go into the shower. "Just a minute," John said. "We're going to be at church all day. We should be back around two o'clock."

"Sounds fine." Dan moved closer toward the bathroom.

"What time are services held today?" he asked.

"9:30 and 11:15, why?"

"I think I'll try to come by for the eleven fifteen service."

John didn't hide his pleasure well. "Splendid. I'll see you there. Oh, and we hold services now in the basement of Tucker Hall. It's a half mile down the road the other way. You can't miss it. It's the tallest building in town."

"I'll save you a seat," Aretha said with a broad smile.

John, dressed in a carefully pressed suit, led the way out the garage. He and Aretha did not take the car; instead, they walked down the lane in the opposite direction of the church.

Dan took a long shower, flopped back on the couch and fell back to sleep. When he awoke, he was completely dry and it was half past ten.

He put on the only pair of pants he brought with him, a pair of Khaki pants that were horribly wrinkled from sitting in the bottom of the bag for a week. He cursed himself for not asking for an iron. He knew they had one somewhere. He searched the house. He moved into the bedroom figuring he would only look around for it, and if it wasn't in plain sight, he would just go with the pants and oxford shirt wrinkled. He found the iron and ironing board in the bedroom already propped and ready for use. Apparently, they didn't have time to put the items away before they left. Dan turned on the iron and waited for it to get hot. While waiting, his eyes scanned the room.

A pair of stockings lay across the bed, but that was the only thing that appeared out of place. The room was in desperate need of painting, but it was sound and had a nice walk-in closet with no door. Dan swung around the room and looked at the worn handed down furniture. It looked like mahogany, but it was hard to see without much light.

He moved toward the dresser to inspect some of the pictures more closely. Dan didn't know the people in them, but based on the close resemblance to John and Aretha, he judged them to be various relatives. The pictures were old, and some were bent, frayed, and yellowed with age. Some were in frames with no glass protection, some were in frames with cracked glass, and still some others in fairly new frames. There were more than a dozen pictures on the dresser alone.

His attention turned to two pictures at the end of the dresser. One in black and white was a picture of John as a little child in front of his parents. The other was a color picture of John and Aretha much younger, maybe even on their honeymoon. John had a polyester suit on and Aretha wore a sleeveless one-piece yellow dress with sunglasses. Both wore their hair natural and John held a cigarette between his fingers. They were in a city, but Dan couldn't guess which one because he could only make out the street behind them and he didn't recognize the buildings or city markers.

He became fascinated with John's past. He had never stopped to see John as being anything more than a minister. The iron began to steam and Dan quickly ironed his pants and shirt. He got dressed and thought about getting a tie from the closet. He turned off the iron, unplugged it, thought better of looking for a tie, and walked out of the house.

It was a drenching Alabama day, sunny and humid. He could see that it was going to be typically hot. The humidity was so thick it hung like a wet blanket around the small hills and flat plains of the area. He was sweating before he even reached the street. By the time he walked to Tucker Hall, his oxford shirt was soaked through under his arms and his back. He was glad he didn't wear a tie. He walked inside the building and was immediately depressed that there was no air conditioning.

Dan saw Aretha up front and he moved toward her seat. All of the people seated were fanning themselves. He was a good fifteen minutes early, so there weren't many people sitting. It was a large old room. Folding chairs were set up and a makeshift pulpit set up front. Music played from an organ in the corner, and a dozen singers hummed to the rhythm. Dan noticed that there was a fan on every seat, and he picked one up as he sat next to Aretha. She was beaming with a beauty he hadn't seen before. In fact, many of the people he saw in the room, many of whom he'd seen working out at the construction site, were dressed up for the services. Some people came over to him and talked to him like an old friend.

Just before the services were to begin, Tarsi approached Dan and Aretha. "Mrs. Freeman, how are you today?"

"Just fine, how about yourself?"

"Fine, ma'am."

"How's your mamma?"

"Feeling better, but Doc Richardson suspects she won't be getting much better," Tarsi said.

"Well, you know I'll pray for you, child."

"Yes ma'am."

Tarsi turned his attention to Dan. "Sir, I've seen you with a few folks playing baseball behind the church evenings..."

"We're going to try and play every day this week," Dan said.

"Well, I was wondering maybe if you have room, maybe I could play with you all some night?"

"How about tomorrow night? We're going to try and get a game going. Are you interested?"

Tarsi's eyes lit up. "Yes, sir. I am."

"Well then, we'll see you out there after work tomorrow."

"Thank you, sir."

Just then music erupted in the room. The chorus sang with a booming voice. The sound was beautiful. Tarsi hurried back to his seat just as an older man began to sing a solo. Much of the first fifteen minutes of the service went this way. A series of songs, with the congregation singing along. The entire congregation was on its feet and clapping to the rhythm of the music. Dan looked around wildly for a hymnal, but didn't find one. In fact, he noticed that not a single congregation member had one. They'd all memorized the songs!

Dan scanned the room and found mostly familiar faces. He also noted that every face was lit with happiness. After the third song, John came up to the podium through a side entrance. When he reached the podium, the congregation sat down.

For the next half hour, all eyes of the congregation were glued on John. He quoted scriptures and talked about life. It was the end of the speech that mesmerized Dan. Up to that point, John's inflection rose and fell as he spoke.

"Now, God has given us much in our lives. We have a town full of goodness, we have a town full of faith, and we have a town full of love for God." John's hands raised high in the air. With every sentence the audience grew louder in affirmation of his praises.

"Are we down because we don't have new clothes for our children? Are we down because we don't drive new cars? Are we down because our homes need repairs, or our children need medical attention? I say we are not because Doc Richardson heals our children for a share of our crops. We aren't down on the Lord because we have people pure of heart and spirit who've donated time and money to help us rebuild the symbol of our faith."

The audience echoed John's crescendo. "One of those men is here with us now, and we welcome him into our hearts and we show him our faith. Life, oh Lord, life is something we cherish. We believe because a burnt church does not mean our faith lies in ashes. It'll take a lot more than that to defeat us. It's what's inside the church, it's what's inside us, that makes that church stand up tall and say yes, we believe in faith and courage. We live by God's example.

"Men who hate, they don't know that. They think burning a church down will destroy the very bedrock of our community, the iron clad will of its faith. But men of hate didn't understand that a building can't be faith. Their mistake has turned out to be our glory for look at how many people have come to show they have faith. This is what we've believed in all our lives.

"These men of hate have led us to our finest hour. An hour where all men and women come together to say they'll endure no more examples of hate, no more examples of prejudice, and no more examples of discrimination. They can burn our church down as many times as they want, but they won't burn away our love for each other!"

John had to stop every few moments to wipe the sweat from his brow with a handkerchief. Despite the fact the doors were open, the room seemed oppressively hot.

"Now, let's bow our heads and pray," John said. "All of us need to pray. We're not going to pray for ourselves now. We have all we can ever ask for in this world. No. We must pray now for those men of hate. We must pray for them because they're missing out on the greatest gift of all. We talk mercy, we talk forgiveness, and these men have never known how to live by those words. They've never known how to live with hope and faith. It's time to take the last moments of our service and pray that someday soon they'll realize what courage is, what real love is, and what faith is. Then we'll have been successful. Then we can shout it from the highest mountaintops, and they'll be there with us."

John fell silent and so did the congregation. Several minutes went by and no one stirred.

It struck Dan like a thunderbolt. In order to continue on the spiritual journey, he wouldn't have to do anything different than what he was doing now. It was so logical. The first step toward having the courage and faith John was talking about was there in front of him. It was a path he'd always taken until recently.

Selflessness. It took the desire to do more for the next person no matter who he was, or how much he seemed to be beyond help. It was the actual motivation to do more for someone other than yourself.

Dan had lived that kind of lifestyle for years. He felt like he was drowning inside because he'd given up his free time to be a parent to his children, to be a husband for his wife. He tried to get back some of this freedom by alienating his wife and children. From his time in Spleen, he had gained the desire to do for others. It could be finding someone to donate five thousand dollars in building supplies to help rebuild a church in the belly of poverty, or walking the dog on a cold snowy afternoon so your spouse doesn't have to. The first step to faith, to the very essence of courage, is to sacrifice for the sake of others. Dan had fallen off that path. He'd revisited the ways of selfishness and had enjoyed it. Now he realized that he'd fled because to live a life of selfishness is the prevention of salvation.

All this entered Dan's mind in the moment of silence. The congregation's example of their ability to be able to forgive someone who'd just tried to destroy everything that made them whole by destroying the very center of their faith would change the direction of his life forever. Like a person exposed to the light after many hours of darkness, Dan was overwhelmed. He tried to absorb as much as he could, but only saw the colored spots that come after being in the darkness for so long.

The service ended. Most of the people left ,

but Dan remained in his seat, a smile across his face.

The sun shone brightly through the windshield. Even with his sunglasses on, Dan had difficulty seeing the road. He looked around the landscape. It was unfamiliar to him, despite having come this way just a few days ago. Dan couldn't get over the magnificent beauty of the land. He was barely aware of his passenger. Matt was silent. He was taking in the scenery.

The exit for the mall approached, but Dan was not conscious of it. Instead, he missed the exit. Dan was caught in his daydream. Matt had to snap him out of it.

They got off at the next exit and a sense of anxiety enveloped them. They made a u-turn in the Center Field parking lot and went back to the Interstate. This time they got off at the mall exit. A few minutes later Dan parked the car and the two were walking in the mall.

The mall wasn't much. It totaled twenty stores, but to Dan it was a powerful reminder of home. It was new, and there were sections still under construction. The two men took their time, looking at all sorts of merchandise. Finally they approached what they came for, a sporting goods store. The store was by far the biggest one in the mall. Dan and Matt walked up and down the aisles looking at the new sporting goods. At last they came upon the baseball equipment. They picked up baseballs, bats, bases, and several types of gloves. They split the expenses, asked one of the clerks for help, and carried the new equipment to the car.

They drove around to the other side of the mall and went into a restaurant. A young blonde waitress with a smile too big for her face sat them in the non-smoking section and disappeared. They studied the menu and another waitress came over to take their order. When she left, Matt spoke.

"I've been thinking of staying here for a few more weeks. I'd really like to see the church when it's completed."

"I don't know what I'm going to do. I need to go home soon." Dan changed the subject. "Why did you come to Spleen anyway?"

"I used to be a really successful business owner. My company grossed over two million dollars a year. There was a price that came with that kind of success. I was insane. Sometimes I worked twenty hours in a day. I never saw my family.

"I lost my wife and one of my children in a car accident a few years ago. They were hit by a drunk driver. The local news covered the story for a while."

Matt's expression changed to one of sadness.

"I felt as if my whole life was torn apart.

Everything that was important was taken away from me. I lived the old adage about never knowing how much you love something until it's gone. I thought that I'd have time for them later. I figured that I would work for fifteen years, retire, and spend the rest of the time with my family. Boy, was I a fool."

"I'm sorry. I didn't mean to pry," Dan said.

Matt returned from his emotional memories. "Not at all. The point is that through all this mess, hundreds of people came to my side. The news ran reports about the incident. Suddenly, people knocked on my door. Some just offered condolences, some offered advice, some brought prepared dinners, some actually gave me money. That was the thing that amazed me. I had more money than I needed, yet here were people who had less giving me money."

The waitress interrupted them by placing the appetizers they had ordered on the table. Matt ate a potato skin before continuing. "Seeing this outpouring of help really moved me. It taught me what was important in life and kept me going. Soon, I found myself giving much of my time to community projects. My son loves to spend the summers at his grandmother's place, so I use that time to do things like this. It makes me feel whole." They ate in silence for a long time. Dan was going over what Matt said. His heart ached for his family. He longed to complete the rest of the puzzle.

Their desserts arrived, and the waitress returned moments later and gave them their check. After paying for their meal, they drove back to Spleen in the calm of the evening.

Chapter 13

Dan awoke on Monday morning well before dawn. He felt renewed, eager. Like a school boy looking forward to his first full day of school, Dan went through his morning routine. Soon enough, the time came for him to head over to the work site. He no longer felt the need to hang on to John and Aretha but instead began moving about the town like a member of it.

The people at the work site were acting differently than usual. Usually the workers would be excited, but this morning was filled with somber news. John and Aretha came up to the work site, and they too had somber faces. Dan couldn't figure out what was wrong, but figured it had to be disastrous.

Dan saw John had a newspaper folded under his arm. At first, Dan felt a tinge of fear and guilt as perhaps the highway incident made its way into the papers.

Dan came up to John and walked alongside, "What's wrong?"

"It's unbelievable," John said, bewildered.

"What is?" Dan was worried. He hadn't seen his friend like this before.

"You mean you haven't heard?"

"Heard what?"

John gave Dan the paper. He moved toward the center of the work force, about forty strong.

Dan sat stunned as he read the front headlines. "Bomb Blast Kills Two at Olympic Park." Quickly, Dan read the article. The glory, courage, and happiness that the town had drawn from the Olympics had been sent spiraling into a vortex of hatred and terrorism.

Dan couldn't believe what he'd read. He was sure it shook the faith of all the people before him. They'd battled so hard against hatred. They'd fought to overcome racism and discrimination through the faith they had in their religion. They had used the Olympics as a symbol of others overcoming the adversity. Now the symbol was scarred.

The sun beat down on them like a vicious enemy. They worked in slow motion. Once again they were broken into groups. Though work was getting done, the vigor and excitement had worn down as bits of information about the bombing continued to be passed around. Wordlessly, the workers continued at their jobs.

More than half of the four by eight plywood sheets had been put up. The church was beginning to be enclosed. It was time for Dan's group to break for lunch. Matt had come up to him to make sure they were still going to play baseball afterward. Gradually, as if coming out of the morning mist into the sunshine, talk began to move away from the Atlanta bombing to the coming baseball game. News spread that there was enough baseball equipment for two complete teams. A sign-up sheet was passed around, and the workers became more animated about their day. By mid-afternoon the plywood was completed and half the building was prepared for the bricklaying. It looked as if they'd be able to finish the brick work by the end of the week.

Dan marveled at their accomplishments. The area around the church had been dragged and was flat and clean. A solemn moment came and work stopped as the debris of the old church was lifted into two dump trucks. Later, trucks delivered the materials needed to make the mortar for the bricks.

The sign up sheet appeared with nearly thirty names on it. Later that afternoon, the owner of the front loader ordered his second dump truck to follow him to the area in which they were going to play baseball. The owner had signed up to play. He consulted with John, who in turn consulted with his congregation. It seemed unanimous, so John agreed to the idea. The machine dug out an infield and put the grass in the dump truck. By the end of the day, the two men dug the foul lines and the rough cut of a baseball diamond. Though it wasn't perfect by any means, it was more than the church could ever hope for.

Teams were picked over pit barbecue. The men got together and stamped out the rough spots and smoothed the infield, outfield, and home plate. It was nearly five-thirty by the time they were satisfied with their makeshift field. Teams had already been chosen, so after a few minutes of warming up, play began.

Matt and John brought the new equipment out onto the field. The grateful members of the town picked the equipment they needed to set up the field and start the game. The historical first baseball game ever played at the church field didn't last more than four innings and was suspended. The Reds, named after the sunburnt captain, had seven, and the Blues five. Tarsi was the hero of the day, hitting two home runs. He displayed a raw talent that Dan hadn't ever seen before in all his coaching of the sport. Everyone agreed to pick up where they left off the next day.

Dan got back to the Freemans' home a little

after nine-thirty. He took a shower, had another piece of fantastic peach pie, and hit the bed like a fallen tree.

He didn't awake until the morning alarm. He was incredibly sore. Previously, all the talk at the site was about the Olympics. Though there was some mention of the games, the talk at the construction site was the baseball game and the small wagers placed on it. A prize of two peach pies was set for the winner.

Most of the work done that day centered around bricklaying. With so many workers, the work went quickly. There were times when too many workers meant that they were getting in each other's way. During those times, some workers could be seen walking toward the baseball field with shovels, rakes, extra plywood, and two by fours. A group of men were turning over the dirt to get to the rich clay. The rakes would smooth it out, then they'd walk over it to flatten it.

To prevent the workers from getting too close together, the foreman spread the workers out throughout the building and laid bricks on all sides of the church. It presented some problems, such as when the corners were connected, but these were neither insurmountable nor time-consuming. By late in the afternoon, the brick work was about a fifth of the way up on all sides.

John stood in the late afternoon heat staring at the creation in process. Dan walked up to him and handed him a plate of barbecue, corn, and collard greens.

"You know, I never thought we'd get this far," John said, tears coming down his cheeks. "I never thought we'd be able to do it."

Dan smiled. "I have to thank you. I came here not knowing what I wanted or what I lacked in my life. I still haven't quite found what I'm looking for, but I'm close. I know I was looking for something, faith perhaps. I see how you have faith despite not having anything else. I see you and I realize that there's nothing else that matters. If you have faith, if you have the courage to continue your life's journey, then the rest will come.

John, tears still running down his face, looked at Dan. "You've given us the greatest gift that anyone could give us. It's you who showed us again where that faith is. Though there were many of us who were determined to triumph over hatred, there were some who were like sheep lost throughout the land, and you were our shepherd who brought us back to the stable.

"When you got here, there were maybe fifteen workers. Some of our members and the townspeople went out to work, but others stayed home. Friends and neighbors didn't care to help. They were afraid. If they depended too much on this one thing, tried too hard to throw their faith into yet another impossible task, then maybe they would fail. That is when you question your faith, whether it be in God or in yourself, and you open the door to a lot of hatred, doubt, and fear. For the first time I can remember our little town withdrew into itself. Then you came, and our people thought it was shameful to have people from other places work on our church while they were home. So we came out, though we doubted our own success. The Olympics suddenly became a shattered dream for us. Your idea to play baseball overshadowed that lost vision, brought us back to our faith."

Dan didn't know what to say. He certainly didn't see his influence anywhere.

Then he realized that he'd stopped thinking about the benefits of what he was doing and had begun to turn his attention to what he could do for the town. Dan felt their vision, he had that faith, and it was all because of his experience with the townfolk. Dan turned and saw that many members of the two baseball teams were warming up. The breeze suggested that an evening thunderstorm was rolling in.

"I have to go," Dan said. "We have some peach pie to play for."

"I'll be along shortly."

"You're going to play?"

John laughed. "No, I'm going to watch. We all are."

Dan turned and saw that some people were at

the field sitting on lawn chairs. Others were sitting on blankets, and still others were standing. Some were smoking pipes or cigarettes.

"The town has many friendly wagers on this game, so you better win, because if you don't, I work on Fred Bartlett's farm next Saturday," John said.

The game started soon after Dan arrived. Dan's team, the Reds, were still ahead seven to five going into the ninth inning. Thunder could be heard in the distance, but lightning hadn't been spotted yet. The breeze picked up a bit, blowing toward home plate.

Dan, who'd been playing third base, saw Tarsi walk toward the plate. Tarsi was a natural baseball player, no doubt about it, but the wind was blowing hard in his face. Dan looked at the runners on first and second. There were two outs as Tarsi stepped to the plate. Tarsi smacked the first pitch thrown to him. Dan stood as he saw the ball climb toward the clouds, saw it disappear like a chameleon against the sky. Then he saw his outfielder drifting back. One figure blurred past him, then another, and Dan figured they were the base runners.

Dan set up the relay for a possible play at the plate. There was none. The ball sailed way over his outfielder's head and bounced once before hitting the base of the newly laid brick work of the church nearly four hundred feet away. Dan barely noticed Tarsi flash past him as his outfielder was just picking up the ball. Tarsi had crossed home plate before the ball made its way back into the infield.

Like a group of people who'd just been informed that they'd won the lottery, the members of the team surrounded Tarsi and jumped up and down. Half the town cheered, while the other half sat in numbed silence.

The two teams shook hands, and Dan saw something on the baseball field he'd never seen before. The two teams got together in front of the area surrounding home plate and prayed. Dan couldn't remember the last time he'd said a prayer, but he knelt down with the group of players.

The wind started to pick up. It was going to be a fierce storm. Still, nobody left the field. Small wagers still had to be paid off, and the peach pies still had to be eaten. Flaunting their trophy in front of the losing team, the Blues devoured the peach pies right on the baseball field. Soon the calls for double or nothing were made and the request of a rematch was set up. It was going to be a best of three series, and the winner would take home ten peach pies. Dan liked the idea. In fact, so did the rest of the town, agreeing to begin working an hour earlier so they could quit by four o'clock to play the games before nightfall.

The storm thundered ominously then, and the entire town made for home. Dan was soaked when he arrived at the Freemans' home, but he didn't mind the rain. He couldn't remember a recent time when he'd been that happy.

Chapter 14

For the next two days the workers played baseball in the afternoons. They arrived early and left the job early. Officially, the work began at the end of April. By the end of July, the outside structure of the church was nearly completed.

During the course of the next two days, Dan found himself working less. He still went to the contruction site, but always found himself talking with John. They went to bed extremely late, falling asleep in the same room because they'd talk to the point of exhaustion. They'd become incredibly close friends.

"You know it's so strange. This feels so comfortable to me, like I always knew this feeling but just forgot about it," Dan said late in the evening.

"You'll find that whenever real love is present, it's comfortable. It's like us. We may never see each other again, but we'll always be in each other's hearts. We'll always remember how much we helped each other's soul, and how we helped each other find peace."

"How did I help you find peace?" Dan said. "It seems to me that you always had it."

"That's where you're wrong. No matter how strong faith is for a person, even for me, the temptation to fall out of faith is always there. It's clinging to the fringes of our being, always ready to take possession of our soul. It's no different for even the greatest and strongest believers. So it was with me. With the responsibility of leading the people of my congregation and this town out of the doldrums of apathy, it was my job to light the spark and set fire to the flames of faith for them. It seems at first we weren't up to the task. You came in and became that spark I needed to lift their spirits. We're a proud town. There's not much that shakes our faith, but occasionally it does happen, and it happened to us before you got here."

Dan picked up his glass of iced tea. "I'm walking toward a new goal, a new light, and I'm scared. You've given me the strength to keep moving on that journey." Dan opened his mouth as if to add something but thought better of it.

"Remember that story I told you about the man

who came to visit me in the hospital? I think the message he was trying to send me was about you. You were the reason I had to wait all these years. One day I'd have the opportunity to save a person's soul, and we did that together. In saving that soul, I just may have saved the soul of this little town. We don't have much, but we do have faith again, and it is because of you that revival has happened."

By Friday morning the talk of the town refocused on the Olympics. They learned to their dismay that the security guard hired to protect the people might have been the one who set the explosive, but the townspeople looked past the Olympic tragedy. The courage of the athletes and their drive to keep their faith in winning inspired them to look beyond the images that could taint that spirit. Their faith and determination was restored by the symbolic reopening of the Olympic park. As the Olympics continued, the townspeople looked past the events and focused on future competition. The town moved toward the completion of the brick work.

Never before had the foreman of the construction site seen people work so hard.

Late that afternoon, talk also turned to the final game of the series between the Reds and the Blues. The series was tied thanks to a 15-8 pounding by the Reds over the Blues.

The sun was still high at four o'clock when

the two teams began to warm up. A table was set up with ten peach pies. Aretha had stayed up into the early morning each of the past two nights making the pies. Unlike the friendships that were evident during the work hours and in the evening while watching the Olympics, the players and spectators were bent on one thing—winning those pies.

After the first three innings of play, the score was tied three to three. Dan's team scored their runs through execution. Dan singled, stole second, and moved to third on a sacrifice bunt that resulted in an error. With Dan on third and a runner on second, the next batter doubled and both runs scored. In the next inning, Dan's team scored a third run when his team got back to back doubles.

The Blues got their runs a different way. With two outs in the bottom of the third inning, Tarsi once again stepped to the plate and ripped a tremendous shot to the opposite field. The outfielder was still running after the ball as Tarsi jogged across home plate.

The sun began to dip below the tree line, leaving only an orange glow in the sky. Unlike the day before, the sky was clear, and Dan figured they'd be able to get two more innings in before they'd have to continue the next day. The Reds scored two more times in the fourth, both runs the results of errors committed in the field. The Reds had their share of errors as well, committing three that allowed two runs to score in the bottom half of the inning. The Reds came back and scored three times in the top of the fifth. Not to be outdone, the Blues scored five times, three on errors, in the bottom of the fifth.

The game was suspended because of darkness with the Blues ahead ten to eight. It wasn't pretty baseball, but it was fun for everyone. Some made plans to watch the Olympics while others had decided to rest.

The Olympics began to quickly fade as the topic of choice. With two more days left of the Olympic games, many of the highlights began to come late at night or early in the afternoon. As a result, most of the discussion about the athletic events centered around the work site. That was where they found out about the women's soccer and softball gold medal games. An old transistor radio hung on the pole in the lunch tent, and the volume was raised to its highest level. The closest people to the radio called out the results, and word spread quickly. Track and Field dominated the evening telecasts, but they were all too tired to stay up and watch. As a result, like the current events of the day, they got their news from that little radio.

Dan sat out on the lawn in front of John and Aretha's house. A swift breeze picked up the front of his hair and blew it to the side. He realized he hadn't gotten a haircut since early

May. He hadn't even noticed how scraggy the sides of his head were. They were beginning to flap in the wind, something he hadn't enjoyed since before he started to go bald. A fleeting thought occurred to him to let the sides grow longer and then comb them over his exposed top. With the way the wind was blowing the sides of his hair, he was sure it wouldn't take more than a month to grow out. He laughed at the vanity of this idea and promised himself to get a really short haircut upon his return.

The night was cool. A cold front had swept down from the northwest. This was completely uncharacteristic of the area, but it was gladly accepted by the rest of the town as a brief respite from the hot summer evenings. Dan looked up and saw the millions of stars. He noticed a few constellations that he knew from grade school, but mostly his mind had difficulty forming shapes out of the stars. He saw a couple of discolored ones and figured they were planets. He never really could remember a time when he saw so many stars.

"Mind if I sit down?" John said, pulling up a chair.

"Not at all."

"What are you doing?"

"Just thinking."

"About what?"

"The stars."

"What about them?" John pulled out his pipe

and put some sweet smelling tobacco in it.

"I can't believe how many there are."

"I say that every time I look at them," John said.

"This is incredible. It's like being out in the woods camping."

"Well, we're sort of in the woods."

"Do you get to see this every night?"

"One of the many benefits of living in a small town."

"Do you come out here often and look out at the stars, John?"

"I come out here often, mostly in the spring and fall, though."

"What do you think about?" Dan said.

"I mull over family problems, community problems, congregation members who are sick. I think about my life, and what it would've been like if that horrible thing hadn't happened so many years ago. I think about God, and how awesome He must be to have created something so beautiful as the sky at night."

John drew on his pipe but still didn't light it.

"I try to think about what it must've been like for Henry David Thoreau to have been in Walden all by himself," Dan said.

"I think about how great we are to have the gift from God to be able to view such beauty and understand it. I wonder sometimes if the animals of the world understand such beauty."

"Could it be possible that we aren't so dissimilar after all?" Dan said.

John pulled the pipe out of his mouth and laughed.

"From the moment I saw you, I knew we weren't that different at all, except maybe if you count skin color."

"I didn't get that impression."

"Because you were looking at me as a member of a religious group. You separated me as a human being based on my religious fervor, but now you have developed that same understanding of faith and you have pulled down the barriers. After you did that, I became similar to you in your eyes."

"I wasn't aware I was doing that."

John laughed again. "That's because you've always been a little behind in the game from the beginning. You were learning the rules while I was already playing."

"I'm going to take off this Sunday."

"I'm glad you're going to stay on Saturday."

"Why?"

"Something special is going to happen."

"What?"

"You'll see when it arrives."

Dan didn't push the issue. "I can't imagine that I'll ever forget what you have done for me."

"Nor will I. I've gone to three different universities, and have received three different degrees, and I have met only one other person that I feel so comfortable with."

"Who's that?"

"A person whom I begged to be my wife. You see, I am a creature of comfort."

"Aren't we all," Dan said, laughing with John.

The breeze picked up a little and the trees swayed under it. They sat in silence for a while, and then Dan got up to go to bed.

"It looks as if we're going to finish the brick work on the church tomorrow."

"It's a good thing," John said.

"What are you going to work on next?"

"I think we're going to start working on the inside."

"How long before the church will be done?"

"It's my hope that the church will be ready to have services in time for Christmas this year."

"That'd be great," Dan said.

"I didn't think it was possible, but lately I've come to understand that anything is possible." There was a twinkle in his eye as he spoke.

Aretha came out of the house with a white shawl over her bare shoulders. "Honey, aren't you cold?"

"No," John replied.

"How are you this evening, Dan?" she said.

"Fine, and yourself?"

"Fantastic. I can't remember when it was so

cool in the summer," She said.

"I was thinking maybe you'd like to go for a walk."

John stood up and looked at her. "I think that's a splendid idea." He reached for her hand.

"I just finished an extra peach pie, if you'd like some," she said to Dan.

"I might eat the whole thing if you're not back in ten minutes."

John and Aretha laughed.

He went into the house and ate a piece of pie with a glass of milk. He wondered how much weight he would've gained if he hadn't worked so long and often during his stay. Then he thought about how fortunate he was to have picked this church, how lucky he was to have found the generous hospitality of Aretha and John.

He decided after shoveling a piece of pie in his mouth that luck had nothing to do with it. He couldn't have been this lucky if he tried.

In the end, he found another piece of the puzzle and it began to make sense to him. He didn't find all these things; God led him to them. It was faith that brought him to this place, blind faith that something wonderful was going to happen here if he came.

As he finished his glass of milk, the aroma of John's pipe began to infiltrate the room as he and Aretha came up the walk hand in hand. Dan shook his head at the wonder of it all, and then a great longing in his heart pounded over him in a huge wave. He realized how much he missed his wife and children.

Chapter 15

The cool breeze that swept through the town had put everyone at ease with a wonderful night's sleep and gave way to the humid day. More than forty people showed up to work. Early that morning, three huge delivery trucks dropped off the drywall pieces and nearly one hundred gallons of drywall paste. The foreman went to Gadsden to rent equipment. Half of the workers spent the morning moving the drywall products inside the safety of the enclosed church. The trucks also brought the tar paper and roofing materials needed to complete that part of the church.

John checked the invoice carefully, made sure that the money was correct, and signed the paperwork. With half of the workers busy putting the supplies inside, the finishing of the brickwork seemed to take longer. It appeared as if they were going to fall short of one of their goals. With the idea of their goal not getting finished, it was decided to quit early and finish the brickwork on Saturday morning.

Dan marveled at the dedication the workers had. Dan was especially impressed with the women of the congregation. They'd become the backbone of the entire construction operation. Dan estimated that almost half the workers were women. They worked on all aspects of the construction of the church, including the framing and bricklaying.

At lunch, Dan saw the women working side by side laying the brick with the men on the scaffolds. Several women played on the two baseball teams. Dan was amazed at how accepting the town was of gender equality. Most of the women were working at the church because their husbands were migrating to different jobs. The church had been a saving grace for the women because it gave them an opportunity to do something besides growing crops and raising livestock. The church was quickly becoming the crown jewel of the town. There was talk of the town fixing up the main street, and maybe repainting the clock tower on Tucker Hall. Because of the loans, the donations, and the time given by all, the church was going to be far greater than anyone had ever imagined.

The baseball game that evening picked up right where it left off. The Blues, which decided to change their name to Franklin's Folly after the name of the woman who was leading the team in hits, was ahead. The game started out with the Reds up first. With the pies laid out in front of them, they quickly jumped all over the pitcher and exploded for five runs in their first at-bat. The sixth inning saw Franklin's Folly go down one, two, three. In the top of the seventh inning, the Reds poured it on with two more runs. They had a commanding five run lead heading into the seventh inning. Once again, Franklin's Folly went down easily. The Reds could practically taste the peach pies. Forcing themselves not to lose their concentration, they added another three runs in their half of the eighth inning. The Reds scored ten runs in three innings and took a commanding eight run lead going into the final two innings.

The first batter walked to start the bottom of the eighth and Tarsi stepped to the plate for Franklin's folly. No one had been able to get him out since they started playing. The teen-ager ripped the ball high into the humid Alabama afternoon. The ball sailed through the air. The left fielder stood and watched because there was no way he was going to get the baseball. The ball struck the base of the church on a fly. The ball bounced off the brick facade and landed in the sprinting outfielder's glove. Tarsi put on a blistering pace, and though the play was close, he was still safe.

Tarsi's team scored six more runs in the inning. They carried that momentum into the field and shot the Reds down. Clinging to a two-run lead in the bottom of the ninth, the pitcher walked the first three batters.

Tarsi stepped to the plate again. The outfield backed up. The pitcher concentrated, reached back, and fired the ball toward home plate. Tarsi swung at the ball as if it were a gnat dancing about his face. The ball rocketed off the bat and was gone from view in a matter of seconds. Dan followed the flight of the ball as best he could. It disappeared momentarily, but Dan knew it was far enough to end the game. The Reds' only chance was that the outfielders were playing much further back this time. The baseball game had divine intervention. The left fielder would've easily caught the ball except that he ran out of room. With an outstretched arm, he abruptly stopped as he hit the wall of the church. The ball didn't hit the base of the wall. Instead, it sailed much further. Dan had never seen even major league ball players hit a ball as far.

With the outfielder helpless to do anything but watch, the ball sailed high over his head and hit the church wall about two-thirds of the way up. Dan estimated that the ball would've traveled well over four hundred feet if it hadn't struck the church wall. The ball exploded off the church and bounced back toward the field. By the time the shortstop ran out for the ball, Franklin's Folly was celebrating its victory. The Reds walked off the field and shook the hands of the winners. Dan felt the crushing blow of defeat. As he looked back at the church wall in the distance, he realized he'd gotten another piece of the puzzle, fortitiude. He smiled and thought it interesting where heroes come from.

Dan didn't sleep well that night. He had a hard time with losing. Even though it'd been a friendly little game, he couldn't stand to lose.

Since Dan didn't get any sleep until much later in the morning, he was late getting to work. By the time he got to the church, the bricklaying was almost complete and there were some townspeople out by the baseball field working on making an outfield fence. Dan also saw a hand-painted sign that advertised for league play. By mid-afternoon the entire brickwork was done. There were still two pallets of bricks left, and the foreman talked of making a brick walkway.

It was a lazy Saturday afternoon. Most of the town sat outside sipping lemonade and smoking cigarettes or pipes. He sat in front of the Freemans' house and longed to be back home with his wife and children.

As the sun dipped down below the horizon,

Aretha came out. Sweat dripped down her forehead as she pulled off her apron.

"Sure is much cooler out here than inside that kitchen."

"I'm sure it is. I don't know how you do it," Dan said.

"Someone has to. Besides, I love to cook. It gives me something to do."

Aretha walked out to the yard and began to prepare a load of clothes to be washed. Aretha was using an antique hand powered washing machine. Dan had seen it the first day he was at the home. It was still working. There was a pedal and a chain. The user stepped on the pedal and the water and clothes circulated in the basin. The water could be released through a plug and was caught in a large aluminum pan and dumped in the wood line a few yards away. The clothes were pulled out of the basin one at a time, wrung through a hand turned wringer, and hung on a clothesline to dry. Aretha had to do the laundry every day as a result of the hot Alabama sun. Dan had to use the device four times. He marveled that a device so old worked so well. The washer had to be close to seventy years old.

Dan found out that it was just one of the many presents given by family members at their wedding. Dan still couldn't understand the concept of family members giving the new couple something used from their own lives. He couldn't believe how close the families were. Dan had never had a close family growing up and often distanced himself from his wife. Though he loved her deeply, he never understood affection. He learned to mask his emotions and rarely showed tenderness. It resulted in many fights in the household over the ten years he'd known her.

"How did you get your name, anyway?" Dan said.

"My Daddy was driving my Mama to the hospital and they heard Aretha Franklin over the radio. My Mama would concentrate on her voice whenever a contraction came. When they saw it was a girl, they just thought it was God putting his two cents in."

"Sure is a lot of faith in God around here," Dan said.

Aretha sat beside him. "Isn't there everywhere?"

"No, there isn't. Where I was raised, I don't think I knew one friend who had faith in any god."

"Well, I always thought that everyone had just a little faith in God. You don't have to believe in God and His wisdom out loud every day. Everyone has ups and downs, but we pick ourselves up, and in the end we always come back to that beginning. So the way I see it, even you had faith just a little bit. Otherwise, how were you able to get where you are now?"

"That's the problem. I'm still not sure where I am, or what I'm looking for. I have so much of the puzzle, but I still can't see the picture," Dan said.

Aretha smiled, patted his knee, and got up. "If that's the case, you have much more understanding than most of us. Most folks don't get nearly enough of the puzzle themselves, but that shouldn't slow down their faith. It should intensify it."

She walked back toward the washing machine, then came back. "John asked me to tell you that he'd like you to go with us into town tonight. We're going to the soda fountain shop for some dessert and to watch some of the Olympics. Will you join us?"

"I'd love to," Dan replied.

"Dinner should be ready in about ten minutes."

As usual, Dan ate his entire meal plus a second helping. He insisted on cleaning the plates, a ritual he had started since their first dinner together. He worked the plates clean, scrubbing the grease off them. When he was finished, he went into the bathroom, freshened up, and was ready to go out with the Freemans. The Freemans were dressed elegantly. John wore a suit and tie and Aretha wore a black sun dress with flowers on it. Dan was woefully underdressed in navy blue shorts and a white polo shirt.

"I'm sorry. I don't have anything nice to wear," Dan said.

"Just because we have a tradition in our small town of dressing up to go out doesn't mean every place in America does the same. You look relaxed."

Dan rolled his eyes. "Well let's relax on over to town, shall we?"

It was a short walk to the town. They arrived at the restaurant. Dan still didn't know its full name and felt embarrassed. Despite the fact it was still dinner time and John and Aretha suggested going to the restaurant, it appeared to be closed. They entered the dimly lit restaurant.

The lights went on and a collective "Surprise!" thundered across the room. Dan was breathless as various members of the congregation came up and patted him on the back or pumped his hand. The room was a whirlwind of activity. Somehow, he found out that John had planned the event. He was ushered to a seat at a table facing the rest of the room. The members of the congregation sat down, and the room became strangely quiet. John stood up and began to speak.

"This may have been my idea, but I want to say not a single person objected to what we're doing tonight. We're throwing a going-away party for a dear friend. He came to us a stranger, but he is leaving us as a member of our community. He is a true friend of the congregation."

There were shouts of affirmation.

"Many of us were sitting in our homes two weeks ago with no direction," John said. The evil of apathy had taken control of our lives. We didn't know how to deal with it, though some of us tried. Then our friend Dan came to our town to help us build our church and that was the spark we needed.

"Now our friend is going to leave us. He's found a faith he hasn't known in his life, and he's humble about it. He believes we've given him far more than he has given us. Tonight, we hope to balance the scales. Tonight, we're going to point out to Dan that it simply is not the case. First, we have a few presents to give out. Dan, this is from the congregation to you."

John stepped off the podium and brought up something that looked like a brick wrapped in white paper. John gave it to Dan, and he opened it. It was indeed a brick. Dan turned it over.

"The plaque reads, *The first brick in this walkway is dedicated to Dan Meridian. May we all walk proud and full of love, like his example,*" John said. "We're going to place that brick in the center of the front path to the church in your honor."

Dan held back the tears.

"We decided that this would be the best way to remember you." John turned toward the front of the restaurant. All eyes followed him as two people came into the restaurant carrying a baby tree with much effort. "This tree, along with another, will stand on either end of a garden on the side of the church near the ruins of our first church. The garden will remind us of the first church, and that there's always happiness after sadness. The two trees will remind us of the two men who came from great distances to help a small town that forgot what love was."

Dan couldn't control the tears. He looked at Matt, and he too was crying.

John pulled out a long flat object, once again wrapped in white paper. Dan opened the present, and stared stunned at the sign. Dan shook his head. "I don't know what to say."

John touched him on the shoulder. "My dear friend, it is we who should be thanking you." He grabbed the sign out of Dan's hand and raised it high above his head. The congregation roared its approval and Dan began to laugh as the tears ran down his cheeks. The sign read, Meridian Baseball Field.

Though Dan was touched by the incredible gestures of good will, he wasn't ready for the next part of the evening.

"To show you that you are indeed a member of our family, and that you'll always be a member of our congregation, some of us want to thank you in our own special way."

One by one members of the congregation said

something to him, mostly of thanks. They came up to his table and each one of them left something behind. Like the wedding tradition, the people of Spleen, Alabama were showing their appreciation the best way they knew how. They were giving Dan a piece of themselves, a piece of their family, a piece of their heritage. Dan was touched beyond words, as one by one, more than thirty people came up to the table with some small heirloom to bring back with him.

Finally, after more than an hour had passed, the procession began to wind down. Tarsi was one of the last people to step forward. He didn't speak that much while Dan had known him. He presented Dan with the game-winning home run ball. It had a red scuff mark where it'd hit the upper tier of the brick wall.

"Finally, Aretha and I had a difficult time figuring out what we could give you. We've been struggling with this for many nights. You've come to mean so much to us. We've opened our hearts to each other, and that is a bond that no gift, no matter how symbolic, can represent. I hope we have come close to that in our selection at least, and we hope you will accept this with your heart. You have earned the right to have this.

"This Bible has been handed down in our family since eighteen forty-five. It's a bit tattered, but it's come to be one of our most cherished possessions. It's our hope that it'll become one of your most cherished possessions through time as well."

Dan stood up. "I don't know what to say."

"Just say thank you," John said.

"Thank you. I mean that. I really do."

"We know you do."

Dan took the Bible from John delicately. Dan sat the rest of the evening numbed by kindness, paralyzed by regret for leaving, and his spirit filled with love.

Chapter 16

The sun slowly exposed itself to the new morning. Dan stood outside and watched the whole sunrise. He'd been out there all night.

He was upset in a way to be leaving. He still held the sign with the field's name on it and the Bible was in his lap. He cherished all the pieces from the townspeople's lives. It came time to say goodbye. He felt a great ache in his heart for his wife and kids. He looked forward to getting back home and to hopefully repairing the damage he had caused.

The sun began to change the color of the sky to a bright orange hue. He sat and marveled at the beauty. In a few moments he'd go inside and he would eat breakfast with the Freemans for the last time. A part of him tried to convince himself that he'd come back again someday. Deep down inside a sickening doubt made him think otherwise.

Dan went into the house and was greeted immediately by the sweet aromas of baked ham, sausage, maple syrup, peach preserves, and grits. John and Dan ate huge quantities of food and Aretha kept serving them. Finally, when they could eat no more, Aretha joined them. There were plenty of leftovers. Dan sipped his cup of coffee. "I think I'll go see Reverend Harper at his church today before I leave. I haven't seen him since I arrived here, and I want to thank him for giving me directions to this part of town."

John looked up from his cup of coffee. "Did you say Reverend Harper?"

"Yes, at the old church at the edge of town."

John and Aretha exchanged curious looks.

"Reverend Harper's been dead for ten years," John said. "That church hasn't been used since then. It's on private property now. We tried to buy it from the owners when the church burned down, but they refused to sell."

Dan sat stunned. "I swear I saw him. He was in his air conditioned room. He gave me directions and everything."

"Old Reverend Harper had an air conditioner, but that went with him when he died. I'm surprised that church hadn't caved in, it's so rotted." John excused himself and got dressed.

Dan tried to compose himself by once again

insisting on doing the dishes while Aretha got ready for services. It took Dan nearly half an hour to clean all the plates, pots, and pans. When he was finally finished, he barely had enough time to get ready.

The plan he had mapped out for himself was to go to the seven-fifteen service and try to be on the road by nine o'clock. He stuffed his clothes into his bag and threw it in the trunk, then looked at the baseball equipment within it, smiled, and hauled all the bats, balls, and mitts out of the trunk. He placed them in the garage and got back to his car before John and Aretha got out of the house.

He met them at Tucker Hall. The service wasn't exactly what Dan had seen the week before. John was more somber, and Dan couldn't help but think it was because he was leaving. The service ended a bit early, and one by one the people in the packed house lined up to hug him or shake his hand.

Matt moved toward Dan. His smile didn't hide his tears well. It wasn't clear to Dan what Matt was looking for, but he'd learned a lot from him. Matt worked hard on the building and seemed as much a part of the town as Dan. Dan saw the goodness in Matt, the pride in his work, and the kindness in his heart. Dan had learned much from Matt's silent example. He would never forget him.

"Goodbye, friend," Matt said.

"I don't know what to say. I'm going to miss

you."

"You've said enough," Matt said.

"If you're ever near Baltimore..."

"If you're ever in Kansas City..."

They hugged each other. Their embrace was strong and heartfelt.

At last Aretha approached him. She had tears in her eyes and a plate with tin foil wrapped around it. She pulled a piece of the foil back to reveal one of her peach pies. He could do nothing but laugh.

"I can never forget you," Dan said. "Of course you can really do me the favor and give me the recipe for that pie, and I will really never forget you!"

"It's all up here," she said pointing at her temple. "Good bye. Take care of your soul. That's what you can do for me."

"I will. At least I know how to, anyway."

She left him and John came forward. He had his hands stretched out, but when Dan reached for it, John was overcome and he pulled Dan into him and the two hugged for a long time. It was as if they were trying to imprint the moment in their memories forever.

Dan pulled back toward his car.

"Right," John said.

With a heavy heart, Dan forced himself into his car. If he didn't leave right then and there, he never would be able to. Without looking back,

Dan headed out of the town the same way he came in.

Chapter 17

Reverend Harper's church looked nothing as Dan remembered it. The church was completely condemned. The grass grew high, the white paint peeled completely off, and the church doors swung open. The roof on the right side was completely ripped off.

He walked up the chipped steps and into the church doorway. The pews he remembered seeing were gone. The church was empty, including any sign of an altar. Dan took two steps into the church with the intentions of going to the back, but the creaking floorboards sent a warning. He stood at the doorway for a long moment, trying to remember that day, but found the events becoming harder to recollect. He shrugged it off and began his journey back home.

When he finally reached the interstate and began heading back toward Gadsden, Dan realized that he had found the last piece of the puzzle. He'd finally figured out that it's not he who controls his destiny, but in large part it's a collaboration of the elements of faith, love, and Him.

Heat pounded through the windshield and soaked Dan's shirt. At about four o'clock in the afternoon, tired from so little sleep recently, he decided to rest for the evening. He pulled into a hotel and settled in for the night.

The air conditioning felt bitterly cold after being outside all day. He opted to eat in the hotel restaurant, sipped some beer at the bar, and caught the baseball scores on television. Then, as the sun began to settle, he went out to the pool. He truly felt rejuvenated. He grabbed a soda out of the machine and settled into his room. He put on the Olympics in time to see the crowning achievement of the games, the women basketball team's victory. He caught the entire second half of the game and the closing ceremonies. Then, with his heart full of trepidation, he picked up the phone and called his wife.

"Hi," he said when she picked up.

"Hi."

There was an awful silence and Dan didn't know what to say. In the back of his mind he worried that she'd given up on him and he was out of her life forever.

"I love you," he said.

"I love you, too."

"Honey, I'm sorry. I realize that now. There's so much I want to tell you, so much I want to say."

"We'll get through it."

He could hear the tears through the phone, and he felt the longing for her.

"I'm going to try to get home as soon as possible. I'm just so tired," he said.

"Take your time. I don't want you to get hurt."

"There's so much I have to tell you about this trip. So many great things."

"I'll be waiting for you when you get back. Honey?"

"Yes?"

"It's going to still take time. It's not over, you know."

"I know it isn't, but I'm going to make this up to you. I'm going to love you with all my heart for the rest of my life. Soon, this will all be a distant memory."

"It's going to take time," she said.

"Are you willing to give me the time?"

"Of course I am."

"Then we have nothing to worry about."

"I love you, Dan."

"I love you."

When morning came, Dan ate breakfast, checked

out of his hotel room, and resumed his trip back on the road. By mid-morning he was in southern Virginia. He passed the spot where he was given a traffic violation for using the emergency turn-around. Suddenly, he pulled off the side of the road and pulled the ticket out of the glove compartment. His court date was set for that day, and it was in two hours. He decided to fight the ticket.

When he arrived in the town, it didn't take him long to find city hall. It took some arranging since he didn't send in his plea ahead of time, but since it was a small town, it didn't take much work.

At a quarter to two, he walked into the courtroom and waited for his case to be heard. A half-hour later, the clerk called his case number. The officer who gave him the ticket was present.

Dan felt his heart racing as he addressed the judge. "Your honor, on the evening in question the officer did indeed pull me over and gave me a citation for using the emergency turn-around. At the time the officer asked me a question that I was unable to answer. I'd like to do that now if I may."

"You may," the judge said.

"Your honor, that evening I was at a cross-road in my life. I was on my way to a place. I was scared, your Honor. Scared of what I might have lost forever because I couldn't find it. I was afraid I'd lost my faith. I'd never before counted on God for anything, and now I had to. I turned around because I was running away from it. The officer asked me if it was an emergency. It was indeed an emergency. I was searching for my soul, and I was afraid of not being able to find it, so I turned around and fled."

There was silence in the court room for a moment.

The judge leaned forward. "Did you find it?"

"What?" Dan said.

"Did you find what you were looking for?"

Dan smiled. "Yes sir, I found what I was looking for."

The judge looked serious. "Good. Fine doubled for wasting the court's time. Next case."

The judge banged his gavel. A moment later Dan was in front of the court cashier, writing a check for one hundred and sixty-seven dollars.

He left the courthouse and walked to his car. The sun was still hot, despite the fact that it was getting later in the afternoon. He pulled out his keys and opened his car door. A blast of hot air met him, and he cursed himself for not putting the sun reflector over his front windshield.

Just as he was about to slide in, he noticed something on the windshield. He pulled it off to get a closer look at the piece of paper. It was a twenty-five dollar fine for parking in a spot with an expired meter. He looked at the meter and saw that he had seven minutes left. He began to look around for the meter maid to protest, but remembered the doubled fine and decided it'd be a fruitless effort. He got in his car and pointed it toward the interstate.

He decided to head east, toward the shore. The sun was setting when he pulled off the interstate and got a hotel room for the night. He drove to the seashore and ate at a seafood restaurant. He walked along the shoreline for an hour. He waited for the sun to set before heading back to his hotel room. Gradually he fell asleep, not caring what time he got up.

It wasn't until one o'clock in the afternoon the next day that Dan got back on the road. He figured he had about another eight-hour drive without stopping. Realizing that he'd get home pretty late anyway, he decided to take his time. He stopped frequently along the way home. At twelve-thirty that evening, he entered the Washington D.C. area and continued on route 495.

He turned off 495 and headed northwest on Interstate 270. At around two o'clock in the morning, Dan entered his hometown of Frederick. He was tired. The only thing that kept him going was the adrenaline rush of seeing his wife when he got home. He couldn't believe he was almost there. He felt as if he'd been away much longer than he really had.

The light was on at his front door. He opened the door, leaving all of his belongings in the car. The lights were out in the house, and there was no sign that anyone was up. Dan went to the refrigerator and then began to brew some coffee. Next, he went down in the basement to the family office. He turned on the desk lamp and pulled out the parking ticket and checkbook.

Suddenly, his wife leaned over and handed him a cup of coffee. She sat down on the chair next to him with her own cup. There was a long awkward silence. Then Dan leaned over and kissed her gently.

"You look beautiful this evening," he said.

She didn't reply at first. Then she smiled.

"Flattery will get you everywhere."

"In that case, you look stunning in that robe."

She nudged his arm playfully.

"We have a long way to go, but we are still together, we are still a couple. We can conquer anything with that kind of love and faith," he thought to himself.

"How did you get two tickets? One for parking in Virginia?"

"It's a long story," he said wearily sipping the mug of coffee.

"We have all night," she said holding up the

cup of coffee and taking a sip.

He took her into his arms. "In that case, it all started when I was thinking about going to the shore, so I turned off into an emergency U-turn."

"Why did you do that?"

Dan looked at his wife with an intensity that'd been absent for years.

"If you ask a lot of questions, we'll never get done with the story," he said with a sparkle in his eye.

"Anyway, I was afraid, but then I met this very kind man, John Freeman."

"John Freeman?"

Dan began to tell his story, but in the back of his mind all he could really think about was how great his life was now that he'd found the faith to face each challenge a new day brought.

Somewhere in the far reaches of time, John Freeman sat sipping a glass of whisky, thinking on the same subject.